The Pobblebonk Earth Detective Club

Going Wild

Sue Baker

Balboa Press books may be ordered through booksellers or by contacting:

Balboa Press
A Division of Hay House
1663 Liberty Drive
Bloomington, IN 47403
www.balboapress.com
1 (877) 407-4847

ISBN: 978-1-4525-3123-6 (sc)
ISBN: 978-1-4525-3124-3 (e)

Print information available on the last page.

Balboa Press rev. date: 12/30/2015

BALBOA PRESS
A DIVISION OF HAY HOUSE

DEDICATIONS

Dedicated to Garnet Baker who taught me so much about the world over the breakfast cornflakes and to Beatrice Kearney, the finest geography teacher a kid could ever have. Thank you both for inspiring my love of learning, travel and of the world.

Thank you also to the world's most special dog, Bentley who has brought so much love and happiness to so many people. Bentley inspires the character of 'The Phantom' in this book.

CONTENTS

PREFACE

In winter Beatrice Kearney wore a fox fur around her neck – complete with the head! My geography teacher, Beatrice had a great passion for her subject. Tall and skinny, her beady little eyes could give a girl answering a question wrongly the most *evil* look. When no one could answer her questions she would accuse of us of 'sitting there like rows of cabbages'. But she made learning interesting and fun.

Of course I became a Beatrice Kearney myself. That is, without the fox fur. But I breathed her fire and brimstone to my students, earning me the nickname of 'Dragon Lady'. Watch out if you don't know your stuff! Beatrice would have been so proud.

After my schooling I couldn't wait to go and explore the places Beatrice had taught me about. Top of my list was the African savanna. Here my love of nature grew into a life-long passion. On my many journeys to Africa I have camped by a waterhole that was home to fifteen hippos and canoed down rivers laden with both them and crocs. Can you imagine my astonishment at finding hippos wandering the street at night in an African town?

Not to mention my amazement when I decided to go walking with ten month-old lion cubs. I imagined cute little creatures. But their feet were already far larger than my hands. Lying in my sleeping bag I have even felt the ground vibrate from a lion's roar! And then there was the time when I went 'wild walking' in Botswana. All that the guide had for protection was a stick! Was I ever scared? You betcha. But I learnt that being scared and meeting challenges is good for your personal growth.

Add to this, climbing volcanoes, walking on glaciers and hot-air ballooning over Turkey. I've experienced being in a sandstorm in the Sahara Desert. That wasn't as frightening as being caught in a small outrigger canoe in a wild storm in the South China Sea. My adventures have taken me all over the world. But everywhere I go, my mission is to learn as much as possible. My study is stuffed to the ceiling with books, maps and photos.

During my travels so many people have asked me where I come from. When I say Australia they look puzzled. Then light dawns – oh 'Orstria' they say, that little country near Italy.

'No guys, you're 14 000 km off target! Try right down at the bottom of the world, 'Down Under'. Yes, there *is* a country down there! Australia is the world's sixth biggest country, with so many special places. And you've never heard of it!'

The world is an endless place of wonderful things to explore, experience and learn about. Yet, so many people know so little about it. How can we live in the world without knowing basic things about it? What about you? How much do you know about this planet?

Through the Pobblebonk Earth Detective Club I wish to open children's eyes about the world they live in, beginning with Australia. So come on kids what do you want be – Earth Ignoramuses or Earth Detectives?

INTRODUCTION

Ozzie, Fee and Pete Mathieson, children who are a 'little on the unusual side', are living a comfortable and happy life in Sydney. But their lives are turned upside down when their father dies. Unable to manage the children on her own, their mother sends them to live with their granny.

Plucked out of their comfort zones, the kids are thrust into a totally alien way of life on Granny's farm known as The Pumpkin Patch. Located in northern New South Wales it is near a village named Frogsville. The children find themselves as social outcasts after utterly disgracing themselves at the Frogsville Show and in their first week at school. Will they *ever* be able to get on Frogsville's good side?

Bored, lonely and miserable, their situation changes big time when Granny takes them on a frog hunt in her rainforest. Exposed to the world of nature, they become fascinated. Hey, this is a whole new world, even better than TV! When, as a result of this, they establish the Pobblebonk Earth Detective Club, their lives change forever.

Which Pobblebonk Detective will become the subject of state-wide news broadcasts? What is it that the children do that leads to near arrest?

The children form their club just at the time when Granny, a mad geographer and adventuress, is wracking her brain for a solution to their problems. Driven mad by their behaviour at times, she thinks it might be an idea to send them to the salt mines in the frozen wasteland of Siberia! Having received an inheritance however, she supports their venture as part of her 'Grand Plan for the Mathieson Children'.

Pete, Fee, Ozzie, The Phantom and cranky old Humph

Part of Granny's plan involves the kids learning about the world through her Breakfast Quizzes. Soon Frogsville School becomes involved too. In fact, the quizzes play a big part in turning things around for the children. You too can try your luck with Granny's now famous and sometimes testing quizzes.

Meanwhile the Detectives' work leads to a number of somewhat bizarre cases and adventures. Some of these cases will have the people of Frogsville gasping in horror.

As the children set up their club they delve into the world of frogs and amphibians. But during their investigation a hideous and poisonous creature appears on the scene. Frogsville is up in arms. Granny's horrible neighbour, an old grump named Humph, has blamed her for the arrival of this menacing creature. The children must solve the issue of who is responsible in order to save Granny.

Poo Dunnit? – the children's first official investigation leaves the residents of Frogsville gasping with shock. It involves the unspeakable subject of animal poo. The kids become wrapped up in the world of scats and tracks in a race against time. Humph has blamed Pete's precious dog The Phantom, for killing his chooks. Will The Phantom be saved? Humph is determined to *get* this family come hell or high water.

During the case the children find a number of lesser-known Australian animals living in the forest at The Pumpkin Patch. They have never heard of any of them. This leads to a detailed look at Australia's weird and wonderful animal life, at creatures found nowhere else on earth.

Next the children become involved in a case concerning a rogue animal that is terrorising boats in the Prince Regent River of northern Australia. Delving deep into the world of reptiles can the children ensure that the right perp is caught?

Perhaps the most bizarre case of all occurs in Chapter 9 – *Poo Dun the Break In*? Some rats 'hold a party' in Humph's kitchen. Humph wants to spread poisonous rat baits *everywhere*. The children apply the principle of 'do not convict until firm evidence is in place'. This steers them further into the world of Australian animals, unearthing more native animals that no one in Frogsville knew existed.

Each case presents Detective Activities that all kids can do. But be warned – you will have to get 'down and dirty'!

CHAPTER 1: LIFE AT THE PUMPKIN PATCH

POBBLEBONKS AND MANIACAL CACKLE FROGS?

'Don't look at me. I ain't got no relatives with names like *that*.'

It all began with ten words, changing the lives of the Mathieson children forever.

'I'll take you hunting for Pobblebonks and Maniacal Cackle Frogs,' their granny said.

'Boppleponks?' Pete asked. 'I know you've been up in Queensland catching those revolting cane toad things but have you been smoking them too? Are you bonkers?'

'No. Wait and see. The rain will soon clear,' she said, gazing out the cobwebbed kitchen window to the rolling green hills. 'Then it will be a perfect time to hunt for them.'

'Come on Gran, you're makin' it up. What self-respectin' creatures would have names like those?' Ozzie said.

The kids had no idea what Pobblebonks were. In fact, looking back later they realised they knew nothing much at all.

'Besides, can I have something to eat first?' Ozzie asked. 'It took a zillion hours to drive here. Hell's bells, I ran out of food before we even cleared Sydney!'

'I don't know how you could even think of food with that stinking dog in the car,' Fee complained. 'How can any self-respecting dog let out a pong like that and not even open an eye to see if anyone caught him out?' Pete's dog, The Phantom, was a black Staffordshire Terrier. Born as the runt of his litter, he had health problems. The worst was that after eating, his stomach blew up producing the most extreme-smelling gas. The Phantom got his name from the 'carpet slippers' he let off. You know, the kind of smell that suddenly whacks your nostrils without any warning.

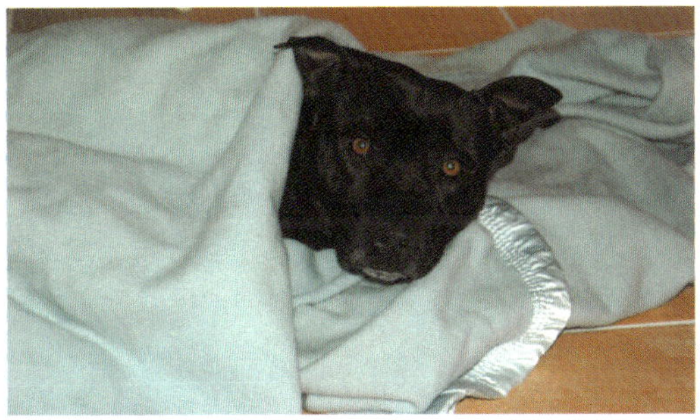

Yeah that's right, blame all the smells on me. I'm just being a dog and doing what all dogs do.

Ozzie threw himself on the blue velvet lounge like a tired rhinoceros. A puff of dust burst from the impact. The lounge groaned. Lounges always did under the assault of his huge buttocks.

'That is so gross,' Fee said looking at his newly grown armpit hair that peeked out from his sleeveless shirt. 'You should wear something to cover it up.'

'And if you don't put on deodorant soon I'll have to wear a gas mask,' Pete added.

Ozzie thumped his chest and looked Pete's skinny body up and down.

'You're just jealous. Anyway I'm not gross. My mates have all got this hairy stuff. *And* they're also sweating like pigs all the time and have blackheads all over their noses. All twelve year old boys have these things it seems.'

Oh dear, Granny thought wearily. Is this what it's going to be like?

That night the kids sprawled out on the musty-smelling patchwork quilt covering the huge old four-poster bed in Ozzie's room.

'Geez come on guys. Please be generous with your donations. Can't you see I'm starving?'

'I tell ya, Granny can forget that frog hunting stuff,' Ozzie complained. 'I'm on light duties this week. I've got a long choco-date and lots of lounge lizarding to catch up on. Besides which I have a massive bellyache,' he moaned, clutching his big tummy. 'And I just know this bellyache's gonna be around for at least a week.'

'I'm not going either,' Fee said, screwing up her big green eyes. 'I'll have nothing to do with it, such a *ridiculous* idea. You can catch warts from those things. And what about those gruesome leeches out there?'

'Aw go on,' Ozzie replied. 'Ya know a leech only needs one good feed of blood a year. Think of it as a donation to the Leech Blood Bank.'

'We've got more important things to worry about. Like, my career is in tatters. How can I possibly further it in this hell hole?'

'You've got such tickets on yourself,' Fee said. But Ozzie *was* talented. The proudest moment in the school's history, his principal had said, was Ozzie's first performance at the Sydney Opera House.

'What about my beautiful clothes? I've got nowhere to wear them,' Fee sobbed. 'I've got no friends here. And how could I tell my old friends that I'm now living on a farm known as The Pumpkin Patch? Or worse still that it's near a village with the ridiculous name of Frogsville?'

'I'm more worried about living with Granny,' Pete said, creasing up his angelic face and running his hand through his curly, blond hair. 'I don't know what we'll be in for. And what do we tell people when they ask what she does? Do you know she's going to write a book about how to track animals from their poo?'

'Anyway one thing's for sure. It seems all we've got is each other for the time being. I think we should try to be nicer to each other.' Ozzie and Fee pondered this. Maybe Pete was right. The kids snuggled up together for the night with Phant at their feet. He thought he was in heaven with so many smelly feet to lick.

With no familiar city sounds like traffic and sirens to comfort them, the kids fell into an uneasy sleep, dreaming of floods and frogs and pumpkins.

How life could change so quickly! It was bad enough when their father died from a heart attack. But then their mother couldn't juggle her work and look after them too. Imagine how they felt when they were shipped out from the bustle of Sydney, Australia's biggest city, to a farm in the middle of nowhere. 'Woop Woop' Australians call it.

But this turned out to be nothing compared to the series of bizarre events that lay in store. Who would have dreamt these kids would become famous? Sometimes for doing good things, other times in disgrace. So maybe that word should be infamous (or 'bad famous').

But those wretched frogs were loving every minute of the downpour

TRAPPED IN A PSYCHO MOVIE

Rain hammered endlessly on the corrugated iron roof again the next day. The rusty gutters of the eighty-year old farmhouse overflowed. Spilling through masses of tiny holes, the rain formed a curtain of mini waterfalls. Zillions of insects hatched in the steam, attracting an army of frogs now plastered onto the windows.

'I feel like I'm trapped in some psycho movie,' Ozzie said, watching a group of sodden kangaroos. They look as forlorn as we do he thought.

'Listen,' Ozzie said, as he hammered his fist against the glass. 'Croak, croak, ark, ark, eee, eee. Shuddup, shuddup you mongrels.'

Miserable and angry as yellow crazy ants, the kids had nothing to *do*. Ozzie paced up and down almost wearing the polish off the floorboards. He turned his time to rehearsing his latest comic routine and some operatic songs.

'You sound like you've swallowed a trumpet, an out of tune one at that,' Fee complained.

'I'm *so* bored. Ain't nothing round here except millions of potatoes, pumpkins and cows. I'm just so 'udderly' bored. Even the local cafe is called *The Udder Café*.'

And if the cow hasn't got any milk, it's an 'udder' failure! The udder has four **teats** or nipples that can be squeezed by hand for milking. Today most are milked by machine.

Now all you city slicker kids fess up. Do you know where milk really comes from? Not out of a bottle at all! It comes from a cow's milk bag or **udder**, that's the 'pink bit' on the cow.

'Wow, look at this I found on the Internet. Up in Northern Russia it's so cold that the cows have to wear bras over their udders,' Ozzie said. Fee gave him the usual ticking off. 'But it's true, look at the pictures,' he said. 'The problem you see is that it is so cold that when people go to squeeze the teat to get the milk, the teat snaps off. It's snap frozen!'

'Geez,' Pete said. 'What would you say if you owned a milk bar? Sorry kids, no milkshakes today, the cows tittybongs froze off last night!' He looked out the window.

'Ya know I swear those pumpkin vines have grown two metres over night,' Pete grumbled when they had stopped giggling. 'I'm sure we'll wake up one morning and all be strangled.'

'Can't you just see the headlines?'

KIDS DIE A BIZARRE DEATH: STRANGLED BY PUMPKIN VINES

Pete looked at the unending lines of rolling green hills and the deep valleys between them. 'No point in trying to escape,' he said. 'It would take six months to get out of here.'

'Come on pal. If you're strangled you ain't gonna wake up! Whatya been eatin'? It's all in your imagination,' Ozzie said. But was it?

'Frogsville is famous for its pumpkins you know. They've even got a special name – Frogsville Mash,' Fee said.

'Yeah well, they can shove their bleedin' pumpkins,' Ozzie said. For a brief moment Pete thought he saw a tear in his big brother's eye.

At last there was a break in the rain. The kids put on their rain gear and sloshed along the muddy lanes.

'Let's climb the hill and see what there is,' Pete suggested. And so they did, but it was Pete and Fee who climbed the hill. Ozzie huffed, puffed and staggered – and swore.

Returning home, the kids paced the floorboards once again. Pete stopped to look at the photos of Granny hanging on the wall. His scientific brain absorbed every detail.

'Wow!' he exclaimed in front of the photo of her surfing the famous Banzai Pipeline in Hawaii. 'Wow,' he said again at the photo of her mounted on a camel in some far-off desert. 'Hell,' he said at the one of her skiing down a mountain that looked like Mt. Everest. 'These are so cool Granny. How did you become brave enough to do all these things?'

Granny thought of all the terror she'd faced on her first hot-air balloon ride. Not to mention canoeing down rivers full of crocs and hippos and camping amongst elephants.

'It just takes a bit of courage. You could do it all too, young man. You're just as brave as me. You've lived in that mad city for the nine years of your life. That's braver than anything I've done.'

'I'd need to be so much stronger.' Pete giggled with embarrassment, thinking how clumsy he was. I'm just a gangle of legs and arms he thought, looking down at his spindly legs and knobbly knees. My legs and arms never seem to know where they should be. 'I'd so love to get on a footy team,' he said.

'You'd be lucky to make it onto a nursing home croquet team,' Ozzie laughed.

Granny had even been walking with ten-month old lion cubs in Africa. Their paws were *already* bigger than her hand!

'If you want to grow some muscles, there's a set of Grandpa's old weights in the shed.' Pete's eyes lit up. Maybe Granny was right. If she could face challenges, why couldn't he? He could work out and maybe get accepted onto a team.

Meanwhile Granny was wracking her brains for something the kids could do to relieve their boredom.

'I know,' she said. 'Why don't you go the library and take out some books on bees, ants or frogs? They're fascinating creatures. Or maybe I could show you how to make pumpkin scones. And when the rain breaks we'll go and feed the chooks. That might interest you.'

Ozzie went to his room, locked the door and pounded his hands into the pillows. Bees! Bees! She wants me to learn about bees! I've gone from singing in the Opera House to this! He prayed to the whole universe – help me! Is this what my life is to be – a boy with nothing to do but bake scones or collect chook eggs? I may as well be in a prison.

Help did come for Ozzie later on. But never in his wildest dreams could he have guessed that his life would be turned around by one of these creatures.

Fee, however, was all for the scones. Her goal in life was to become the world's most famous television chef. She raced off to get dressed up.

'It will be good practice for when I get my own show.'

Granny put on her galoshes and took Fee to collect the eggs.

'What was it like?' Ozzie asked.

'Ew. It was foul! It stunk in that fowl pen. Erk, I had to put my hand right into the nesting boxes. *Anything* could have been in there. The eggs were nice and warm. But some had feathers stuck on them and you wouldn't want to know what else too!'

'What is that stink in here then?' Pete looked around. 'Strewth Granny, look what you've done. You've trodden chook poo right through the kitchen.'

'No worries, that happens all the time. I just forget to change my boots.'

DINNER GUESTS

That night the children gathered round the large kitchen table, the hub of all farmhouses. The blackened kettle sang merrily on the ancient wood-fired stove, hissing out soft puffs of steam. Bubbles pinged gently on its bottom. The timbers creaked and groaned as if straining to hold the old house up. Pumpkin scones lined one end of the table.

Fee was still dressed in her practise TV outfit. Her frilly red dress was one thing, but the tiara was another, Ozzie thought. He worked hard to control his laughter.

'Are you pretending to be a Russian Princess?'

Two possums peeked down from the rafters. They were thinking, why don't you put that roach thing with its fierce set of horns in the 'house' with the hairy spider?

'Well you never know. I might just marry a prince some day.'

'At least you're Queen of the Pumpkin Scones,' Pete said as he set about feeding his zoo.

'You're not going to feed them on the *kitchen table* where I'm going to eat are you? Not that filthy rhinoceros cockroach thing?'

'Watch it! Clarence is a *native* bush cockroach. He's a clean piece of work. Not all things that look gruesome are pests you know,' Pete scowled.

'Don't you dare let your wildlife get near my cooking,' Fee said

Pete's frill-neck lizard sat on the table waiting for his dinner. One holiday in northern Queensland, Pete found a goanna raiding a nest. Scaring it away he rescued several eggs, keeping watch over them. One morning they began hatching. Fee was horrified – what on earth were they? Granny confirmed they were frill-neck lizards! They hung around the garden of the holiday house where Pete fed them cicadas and beetles. One of them, Derwent loved to hang out in Pete's backpack.

When the holiday was over, Pete released them into the bush. But when Pete returned home what jumped out of his backpack – none other than Derwent. *No way* was Derwent going to be separated from his best mate.

Derwent

Breathing his fishy-smelling breath, Phant sat *at* the table, grinning with glee. Granny was allowing this for the time being until Pete settled into his new world. But at least the dog *was* dressed for the occasion with a bow tie around his neck. Fee wondered when someone would invent breath freshener for dogs.

I mean how embarrassing is *this* she thought? How could I ever invite a friend over?

Phant waited eagerly to see what was on the menu. Not spag bog please he prayed. We've had that three times in the last week. His nose twitched in anticipation. Granny set dinner on the table. He looked disgusted. Poo dun that? He let go of some gas in protest. It smelled like pure recycled Chum.

'*Must* you do that at the dinner table?' Fee scolded him. The dog feeling most offended, hung his head.

THE BRUSSELS SPROUTS WERE RUINED

'Oh no, not sprouts,' Pete wailed. 'You know what that does to Ozzie. We'll be in for it all night.'

In his sprout-filled despair, Pete forgot to put the lid back on Clarence, the cockroach's house. Derwent took off like a flash after that mouth-watering roach. Phant leapt off his chair and over the table, mad as an angry bull ant. Lizards sent him hysterical.

Fee's scones, all creamed, crashed to the floor. Clarence dived for shelter in the sprouts, letting out the loud hiss for which he was famous. Startled, Derwent plunged into the Frogsville Mash. Phant went for him sending the mash onto the floor too.

'Now look what you've done – all my beautiful scones. And we could catch hepatitis from that revolting roach-thing. You know, the disease that blows up your liver and turns your skin yellow. I hope you catch it anyway.'

'Come on,' Pete pleaded. 'See the good side – I saved us from those awful sprouts! What a lot of trouble I went to though,' he laughed. Clarence was eventually caught and all was restored to order, except the dinner. Granny served up vegemite sandwiches. Phant looked appalled. It's a dog's life as they say.

After dinner, Ozzie complained again bitterly, 'what a horrible, disgustin' day. So stinkin' udderly boring.'

'Maybe tomorrow's Frogsville Show will be a hoot,' Fee suggested.

Oh yes, it would be a hoot all right. The kids would just about be hooted right out of Frogsville! What happened would go down in Frogsville history.

CHAPTER 2: A BAD START IN FROGSVILLE

DISGRACED AT THE SHOW

Saturday dawned bright and clear but Fee woke up with a feeling of dread. Somehow she knew that it was going to be a *bad* day. The kids went off full of excitement. Maybe there would be interesting things to do.

They weaved their way between the trucks, animal trailers, bellowing cattle and whinnying horses that clogged the showground. The smell of pies, popcorn and manure wafted through the air. Phant shook with excitement.

'Dya believe this?' Ozzie asked as they entered the first exhibit. 'A shed full of pumpkins and potaters! Ya call this exciting?'

'And look at the scrawny chickens, all waiting for guys with the Judge badges to decide which of them is best.'

'I didn't know it snowed here,' Pete said. 'Look at all these knitted ski hats.'

'Those are tea cosies – you put them on tea pots to keep the tea warm,' Granny said.

'What do you reckon is in these jars? Looks like rabbit guts pickled in urine,' Fee said.

'Those are preserved plums, the work of Miss Ramsbotham, your new principal. Oh no, look, she's just over there – she's *heard* what you said!' Granny pulled Fee aside, her lips pinched in anger.

'Ho!' Ozzie laughed it off. 'It reminds me of the time I had my appendix out. Remember when Gramps was still alive and I told him I'd lost my appendix? Don't worry, he said. I know where they are – in a jar on the kitchen table!'

Embarrassed and itching to watch the cattle judging, Granny dragged the kids to the show ring.

'Is everyone wearing a uniform?' Pete asked. He gazed round, eyes wide with awe. Men, women and kids were all dressed in blue jeans with big silver-buckled belts, blue shirts, R.M. Williams boots and well-worn hats. He felt very out of place.

'Oh, look at the milk bag on *that* one!' Granny cried with joy, as the cattle were lead around the ring.

The kids couldn't believe how much in love with cattle and chooks all these country people were.

'Oh, look at the milk bag on *this* one. But Granny it's cold enough up here for tea pots to wear knitted jumpers. So where is the cow's bra Granny, you know to stop its tittybongs freezing off like Ozzie found on the Internet?' Pete exclaimed so loudly that all the spectators heard. He was proud to show them that he was grasping onto all this country life stuff. The kids in the crowd howled with laughter. Then a deadly silence fell.

'What's wrong? What have I done?'

'That is not a cow. It is a *bull*. That is not a milk bag. It is the bull's 'you know what'.'

'What's a bull's 'you know what'?' Pete asked even more loudly.

'You total dork,' Ozzie dug him in the ribs. 'It's his 'equipment' for making baby cows. Didn't you hear him say to the girl cow, you're so 'udderly' beautiful?' The kids in the crowd split their sides laughing. Pete hung his head trying to hide his tears. 'Now see that big bull there – he thinks he's a cutlet above the rest! And that one – he's so old he's gonna get the chop! Dya know what you get when you cross a cow with an octopus by the way? A cow that milks itself!'

'*That* bull,' a farmer with a beetroot-coloured face yelled, 'happens to be our *prize* bull.'

The cattle parade was flung into chaos. It took six men to catch that bull and calm it down.

Striding over, the disgusted judge asked Granny, now a shade of fizzy pink, to take the kids away.

'This,' he boomed, 'is Frogsville's most important event. It is sacred. How dare you make fun of it, and of us.'

As they left, Ozzie turned and boomed to the crowd, 'anyway dya know how Frogsville got its name?'

The bull seemed to sense that he was being insulted and jerked violently. Kicking its legs high it broke free taking off like a bucking bull in a rodeo.

FROGSVILLE: Where old geezers come to croak!

WORSE WAS TO COME

'Let's have lunch and then we'll watch the footy match,' Granny said. *Surely* nothing could go wrong there she thought.

Each year at the show Frogsville played the neighbouring team from Comboyne. Over lunch Granny explained that Frogsville hadn't won for ten years. This year the team had new players. Everyone was sure the disgusting record could be turned around. In fact, many bets had been placed.

The game got underway. Frogsville's new players did their stuff. The crowd roared and bellowed. It was a long time since so much excitement had happened. With twelve minutes to go the score was five-six in Comboyne's favour. Surely Frogsville could score one more goal?

Just then Pete joined his family after letting Phant explore all the lovely smells of the show. Phant caught sight of the ball. Hey what's this? Now if there was anything he loved it was balls. He sat up wide-eyed and trembling, every muscle in his body tensing. Suddenly he forced his head out of his collar and bolted over the fence. Like a racehorse he screamed down the edge of field. His little back legs flicked up furiously.

Hang on a minute though. Everyone edged forward in their seats. Frogsville was about to kick a goal! A red headed player lined up the ball, knowing the village reputation relied on this one kick. No way he could miss. Just then Phant saw his chance, swooping in like a flash of black lightning. Grabbing the ball he took off. The footballers chased and screamed at him. But this was Phant's fave game that he played with Pete every day. He ducked and wove and twisted and turned like a pro. He was bowled over with excitement at so many people to play with.

By the time Phant had finished with it, the football looked like it was ten years old.

'Get a gun and shoot him,' someone boomed.

'Get off yer bloody mongrel,' the players roared. But Phant had never had so much fun. Pete charged onto the field. Finally he got within hearing distance of the dog.

'Sit! Drop!' he roared. Sensing that he was in trouble Phant cowered and obliged. 'I'm so ssss… sorry,' Pete cried to the players. He handed the tooth-marked ball, covered in dog slobber to the Frogsville captain.

The crowd was shouting, 'take yer mongrel dog home.' They began chanting in unison, 'go, go, go.' The game resumed but the damage was done. Comboyne won *again*.

THAT WASN'T ALL!

The next day it was time to front up at Frogsville Central School. The kids waited with dread at the farm gate. Some horrible person had pinned a sign to it.

CRACKPOT COTTAGE FARM

Pete clung to Phant, sobbing about the sign and shaking at the fear of a new school.

'What's the matter little one?' the driver asked, as the bus pulled up.

'I don't want to leave my dog. He's my best friend.'

'My dad's comin' round with a shotgun tonight,' a muscly boy with carrot-red hair growled. 'He ain't never gonna forget how that idiot dog ruined his goal yesterday.'

Then the boy began teasing, 'little boy can't leave his dog. And he don't know the difference between a boy and girl cow neither. Where's your doggie's bra eh? Does he get cold in winter too?' Everyone roared laughing.

But then the huge bulk of Ozzie loomed over the boy. Whoa! What was this, a new species?

'What size are ya boxin' gloves pal?' The boy shrunk back into his seat.

Behind the toilet block at lunch time a skinny boy sat and wept into his sandwich. Fee heard the sobbing when she went to the loo. She put her arms around Pete and they wept together.

I think my peace in this beautiful place is ruined forever, Granny thought.

'Why, why, why?' Pete sobbed. 'Why did Dad have to die? Why did we have to come here? Why can't we be at home with Mum?'

'I'm sure things will get better for us,' Fee tried to soothe him. But her day had been beastly too.

That afternoon Granny and Phant waited eagerly at the gate.

'Do you know what happened?' Fee said flailing her arms in the air. 'It was an absolute disaster!'

'Let's have a drink first,' Granny said. She served homemade lemonade on the wooden veranda overlooking the valley. Smoke drifted out of the old chimney. Ozzie licked his lips at the smell of pumpkin soup wafting from the kitchen. Granny listened to the bird song amongst her native flowers and the gentle music of the tumbling creek.

'Well now, what happened?' she asked uneasily, as she settled in the big cane chair. 'Did you by any chance learn some geography today?' A retired teacher, she regarded geography and things about the environment as *so* important. 'They're far too neglected in schools these days,' she complained far and wide. Whenever the 'Big G Word' was mentioned, she just about danced a fandango (that's a Spanish dance).

'Everyone smirked and giggled,' Fee began. 'Fancy *any* kid not knowing the difference between a milk bag and a bull's equipment or what a tea cosy is they all said. So the principal, Miss Isabella Ramsbotham-King suggested we fill out a survey, to help match us up with some other kids and settle in. Ozzie had to list his favourite event as the Pumpkin Pickers' Ball, didn't he?'

'Yeah but you made it worse by listing the Toenail Pickers' Ball,' Pete said. 'And both of them said the Frogsville Sewage Treatment Works was their favourite place.'

'Well? Ain't sewage works good places for bird watching?' Ozzie interrupted. 'I happen to like bird watching. Especially ones with legs like those of Samantha Sneddon-Smythe, that girl in my class.'

'You've got the hots for her haven't you?' Fee scowled.

'She's just a bimbo,' Ozzie said, trying to cover up his interest.

Please don't tell me I'm in for girlfriend problems too Granny thought!

'She's no bimbo. She's top of the school. She's too studious for you anyway. Just remember the principal's comment on your last report card.'

Ozzie's work is outstanding. It is about time he handed some in!

WHAT OLD IRK DID TO FEE

'You're just jealous. Anyway tell Granny what the principal did to you.'

'I told her I was the top student in my old school. She said, well you will just have to prove yourself all over *again* girlie won't you? I can't see how you would ever amount to anything. I doubt you could compete with our brilliant Samantha anyway. I wanted to smack her in the chops,' Fee said, tears of rage and frustration streaming down her face.

'And then the old beast told me I couldn't come to school dressed like I was. She made an assembly announcement.'

'Girls in *my* school will not wear make up and tiaras, especially when they're only eleven years old. If you think you can come dressed like that then you can just come dressed in nothing at all.'

'It was a scream,' Ozzie said. 'The whole school broke up!'

'Do you know what else Ozzie wrote on his survey?' Pete giggled with embarrassment. 'He said the most important thing he learnt in the last year was the length of an elephant's willy. In case you don't know Granny that's over two metres! Old IRK as we've now named the principal, nearly choked reading that bit.'

'Yeah Pete, you didn't help by listing Suggan Buggan and Tittybong as ya favourite places. But IRK hadn't heard of them. She thought they were new swear words.'

'Well you gassed out the hall with your silent-but-deadlies. Everyone was fighting to get window seats. Gran, please don't pack boiled eggs for his lunch. And don't allow him to buy Spam in a Can any more either. And stop making us eat Brussels sprouts too,' Pete said, full of hope.

'It's always hard settling in. I'm sure things will get better soon,' Granny said in a shell-shocked voice. She felt a hundred years old.

'What have you done to your gorgeous long hair?' Granny exclaimed next morning. She eyed off Fee's hair dyed in a multitude of colours and all spiked up.

'Ya look like you've been electrocuted,' Ozzie smirked.

'Well I may as well be, living in this dump. Can't you stop being a mutant and just be nice for once?'

Fee stamped off to school barefoot and in a pair of Pete's school shorts, tied up with a rope belt. Let's see how old IRK likes this she thought.

'How did it go today then?' Granny asked that afternoon, dreading the answer.

'IRK didn't have time to deal with Fee,' Ozzie replied. 'She was too busy with the damage control from Pete's escapade. What do you think crawled out of his backpack at assembly? None other than Derwent! You'd think none of these so-called country kids had ever seen a lizard before. They shrieked so much that Derwent bolted for the safest place, the canteen. Pete and all the boys ran after him.'

'Somehow he got up onto the counter. He stuck his frill up, opened his mouth and sat there glaring at everyone. Honest, he looked like the Creature from the Deep. *Nothing* would make him move. Every time someone tried to slap a box over him he dodged out of the way. So you see, the canteen ladies who were hysterical too, couldn't serve from the counter at lunchtime. It was total chaos.'

Putting up his frill, by the way is the lizard's way of defending himself. It makes him look so much bigger and fiercer. And it looks so fearsome it *is* scary.

THE DREADED INTERVIEW WITH THE PRINCIPAL

One of those pale blue envelopes marked 'Department of Education' arrived. Everyone knew what it would say.
'One thing's for sure. It ain't gonna be no party invitation,' Ozzie said.

Dear Granny,

Please come to the school at 2 pm this Thursday for a discussion about your grandchildren.
Isabella Ramsbotham-King

Would the kids set a world record and be suspended after only one week?

'Please understand that we have problems,' Granny said to Old IRK when she fronted up. 'The children's father died suddenly. Their mother is a university teacher and couldn't manage them *and* her job. The children's wonderful city life has been thrown on its head. They're fighting the change and are determined not to fit in. I suspect they think I will take them back to Sydney if they cause enough trouble. Please give them time to settle.'

Miss Ramsbotham looked bored. She'd heard it all before. Spare me, she prayed. When Granny mentioned Ozzie's talent, she raised her eyebrows, sweeping long purple-painted fingernails through her immaculate silvery-purple hair.

'What, he's got *talent*?' In your dreams lady, she thought. 'I've not seen a shred of evidence for talent, of *any sort*. Except for causing trouble. I'm on the brink of suspending him. He's become an anti-hero. (That's a 'bad' hero, like Ned Kelly the bushranger). The kids love his clowning around and are behaving badly. No one can control them.'

'*Please* understand,' Granny pleaded. 'Their father was a good man, but he had strong ideas about what he wanted in his sons. He didn't believe in boys wanting to act, sing and dance. To him that was girly stuff, a Billy Elliot sort of scene. He wouldn't even watch Ozzie perform. He saw him as a failure, especially after he created chaos at football one Saturday.'

The dream of Ozzie's father was that he should be like this.

'Ozzie tried so hard to meet his father's expectations. It was the day of the semi-final. Ozzie caught the ball without dropping it for once. He looked up and seeing the goal posts just metres away, gave the ball an almighty kick. It flew high through the air, landing beautifully between the posts. This will be my moment of glory he thought! But he was at the *wrong* end of the field and had kicked the ball to the *opposition*'s goal post!'

'You idiot, the crowd roared. *Take him off.* That was it for Ozzie, the last straw. He began overeating, became uncaring about his appearance and started acting out.'

Heaven help me, Miss Ramsbotham thought. I'll need four extra staff to cope, one for each kid and one for me. She wrote on her to-do-list.

Ask Department of Education to provide extra staff to assist with newly arisen social welfare problems. *Urgently.*

NEXT STOP THE SIBERIAN SALT MINES?

Granny was still recovering from all the events. She phoned the children's mother late that night.

'We need a drastic solution. You know, I look at the photo of Ozzie with his dancing trophy taken before he went off the rails. He was so slim and handsome, every mother's dream. I'm sure he's suffering greatly. If only he would open up. Pete embarrassed himself in front of the whole village. And living with Fee's ups and downs is like being on a roller coaster.'

'Why do you think she is so moody?' the mother asked.

'But leave it to me, I'll hatch a plan. It will be my new mission. Perhaps a year in the Siberian salt mines might do them good,' she laughed as she hung up.

'Hmmm,' Granny said out loud as ideas began buzzing around her head. 'Siberia *would* be a good idea.'

Pete had been listening in on his way back from the loo.

Shaking with fear, he woke the others up, 'Granny's hatching an awful plan. She's gonna send us to the Siberian salt mines for a year.'

'I think we have a teenage rebellion coming at full force,' Granny said. 'You know – moods, anger, tears, defiance, zits and the whole bang lot.'

'Oh no!' Fee shrieked. 'That is the place way up in Northern Russia. The one where we read about the cows' teats freezing off! The salt mines are where bad people are sent. I'll show you in the atlas. Fire up the Internet Ozzie.'

The frozen lands of Siberia

'Look at this!' Ozzie exclaimed. 'There's a road up there called the Road of Bones. Thousands of people forced to work building it died from the cold and exhaustion. It was built using pickaxes and wheelbarrows! But there's worse. The skeletons were buried in the road base. Can you imagine!'

All night Pete had nightmares of the pictures they found – a frozen wasteland, bleached white. Despite the hot night, he shivered thinking of the one-month long summer up there. The temperature on an average day was minus 5°C! He thought of the one million criminals banished there to work in the overcrowded, filthy mines. He dreamt of driving that road at night with skeletons dancing all over it. Maybe we should appreciate what we've got he thought. Is life in Frogsville so bad after all?

Later he woke the others again, 'can you hear that noise – clunk, clunk? Is something after us for being so bad? Is someone coming to take us to Siberia? What about Phant and Derwent?'

'Your old fleabag will have to stay here. The Siberians would never allow it, especially after you've fed it those dried pigs' ear things. The air up there is too pure,' Ozzie told him. 'And Derwent would die from the cold. I think you'll find your noise is a frog on the roof, or maybe a phantom pumpkin pincher.'

But could the kids redeem themselves in time? The answer came fast.

CHAPTER 3: A TURN OF EVENTS

A *REAL* INTRODUCTION TO COUNTRY LIFE

Granny was pacing up and down. So too was her cow Milkshake. That meant she was about to 'drop' a calf – Milkshake that is.

'Last time the calf was upside down,' Granny explained. 'It was all most difficult. The calf should have its head at the top of the birth canal. Its front feet should point towards the ground. I'm worried I'll have problems again.'

Right at that moment a yellow water sac burst from the cow's birth canal.

Granny put on a long pair of gloves and rubbed lubricant all over them. She put her arm right up to the shoulder into the cow's birth canal.

'Oh dear, it's upside down again. There's no time to call the vet. You'll all have to help me.'

Fee gulped, Pete went white and Ozzie tried to slink away.

'Don't you *dare!*' Granny said. 'I need your muscle.'

'It's complicated,' she said. 'I have to push the calf as far forward in the uterus as I can. Then I have to pull all the legs into the right position.' She poked and prodded. Eventually she pulled her hand out, covered in blood and guts. 'Quick pass me those chains.' Granny tied the chains onto the calf's front feet using a double half-hitch knot. 'Okay Pete and I on one chain, Fee and Ozzie on the other. When the cow is straining, pull. Let her rest in between. The cow gave several great heaves. 'Pull! Pull.' The kids were pulling – like crazy. Nothing happened. Milkshake groaned in pain.

'Here she goes again. One, two, three, pull again,' Granny gasped. And suddenly out slipped the calf, all covered in muck of course.

'Yea! We did it. How clever were we? And isn't it just gorgeous!' Pete said.

'Can I be its godfather?' Pete named the calf Upside Down.

'It's not over yet young man. The calf isn't breathing yet.' Granny then cleaned out all the muck in the calf's nose. She tickled its nose with some clean straw to make it shake its head. Hey presto! It was now breathing. 'Time to leave mum and baby alone now.'

'But what about all the muck?' Ozzie asked.

'Don't worry. Milkshake will lick her calf clean. It's part of the bonding process.'

Thank goodness humans don't have to do that, Fee thought!

GRANNY'S BREAKFAST QUIZZES

'What's wrong with you?' Old IRK said to Fee who was slumped over her desk the next day.

'Well you see, Granny's introduced us to a daily Breakfast Quiz. I've had to do a lot of study for it. At least the quiz helps us get through the horrible breakfast she serves. Fibre she reckons, it's so good for your bowels. As if Ozzie needs anything for *his* bowels. He reckons this stuff is leftover pigswill that Granny feeds to her piglets. At least poring over the atlas to find the answers keeps our minds off the gunk.'

The class tittered. IRK blushed. But Fee didn't add that Granny's quiz was begun to help her match up to Samantha Sneddon-Smythe. Fee was reading everything in Granny's library. Notebooks and pens were strewn across her room. Reading through everything again early next morning helped her to remember all the facts.

'What was today's Breakfast Quiz about?' IRK asked.

Pete was on messenger duty and had just stuck his head in the door.

'We had to name the world's in…incont..inents,' he stammered over the big word.

Fee bit her lip and put her hand over her mouth, trying not to laugh.

IRK turned brick red and spat, 'I think you mean **continents** or large land masses.'

Pete dodged the torrent of saliva that sputtered from her mouth, just in time.

'You're wanted in the office Miss,' he said.

When IRK was out of earshot Fee doubled over, convulsing with laughter. Her whole body shook. The laughs came out in great whooping howls.

'What? What? Come on tell us,' the class pestered.

'Incontinent is when you can't control your bladder,' she said, wiping the tears from her eyes.

Fee was going to be top of the school, come hell or high water.

'I reckon that's just about how IRK is right now,' someone said.

IRK heard the class roaring from the other side of the quadrangle.

'Miss, is incontinent when you wet yours…?' some one yelled out, when she returned.

'That's *enough*,' she hissed, cutting off the question. She banged her hand so hard on the desk she nearly broke it. The desk that is. 'Let's get on with it Fee.'

'We had to name the Australian states and territories and their capital cities too.'

'What! *Everyone* knows that.'

'Well try it out on the class then.'

'Come on kids rattle off the states,' IRK said smugly.

'Sydney!' someone shouted. 'New Zealand, America.' Not *one* child knew the answers.

'What is the capital city of the state we live in?'

'I know,' bragged the boy with the carrot-coloured hair. 'Queensland!'

'That's a state you dope,' Fee said.

'Who can name the ten other countries of the world starting with the letter A?' she then demanded.

'Africa! Alligator! Arsenal! Arthuritis,' the answers came thick and fast. 'I know, what about Astra?'

'That's a type of car you fool,' Fee snarled, rolling her eyes. 'See, no one knows anything. How come *you* don't know the answers Samantha?' Samantha scratched her head and fumed. How could it possibly be that I don't know the answers to something so simple?

'Granny said your school is an utter disgrace,' Fee said to Old IRK the next day. 'You are breeding a generation of ignoramuses. She wishes she could get her hands on your students and really teach them something.'

Hmm IRK thought angrily. That old bat thinks she's a better teacher than me. I'll get her in as a guest teacher and we'll see. And I'd better do something to get my students up to scratch. Perhaps Fee should do a regular Breakfast Quiz.

THE BREAKFAST QUIZ: AUSTRALIA PART 1

Okay now kids let's test *you* out. Can you pass Granny's quiz? It's been made easier for you, but it's still a whopper. This time Samantha knew six answers. She too was now sitting up all night reading books. The rest of the school came up with only two more answers. What a pack of pumpkin heads they are, Fee thought.

RULES FOR ALL QUIZZES: Answers *may* be looked up but only after an attempt has been made to answer them first. For answers that are looked up score only half a point.

Australia is one of the world's seven large landmasses or **continents**

AUSTRALIA

- Complete the table below. Some hints have been given. Overseas Detectives could draw up a table like this for their own country.

AUSTRALIA

Size in square kilometres: 7 682 300 sq. km; world's sixth biggest country
Longest river: Murray D - - - - - -
Longest mountain range: Great D - - - - - - - - R- - - -
Highest mountain: K - - - - - - - - - (in NSW)
Lowest point: L - - - E - - - (a lake in South Australia)
Population:
Capital city:
Two largest cities:

Refer to the map of Australia above. These are the names of the Australian states: New South Wales, Victoria, Tasmania, South Australia, Western Australia, Northern Territory and Queensland.

- Can you place the name of each state in the correct position on the map? If not, go to the website <yourchildlearns.com> or to Map Snap: Australia at <coolmath – games.com> or another website with interactive map games.
- Which is the biggest state?
- Match these capital cities to the list of states: Melbourne, Hobart, Perth, Adelaide, Darwin, Sydney, and Brisbane.
- Name the capital city of Australia and the small territory that it is located in.

Part 2 of the quiz is located at the end of the chapter.

COMBINED FROGSVILLE SCHOOL SCORE: 8/25 **YOUR SCORE:** /25

IRK GOT DESPERATE

All the classes had a go at the quiz. It was fun they said, far better than boring maths. Ozzie came up with a great idea for Monday morning Show and Tell. He would produce a report on Australia. If that didn't impress Samantha nothing would. On Monday morning IRK let everyone except Ozzie have a go.

'But miss, I've spent all weekend doing this fantastic report.'

'Boy, how could anything you've done ever be fantastic?' IRK retorted. Samantha snickered. Ozzie bit his lips and hung his head. That night he went to bed without dinner.

On Tuesday morning Old IRK strode angrily across the playground. Everyone scattered out of her way. Her purple hair was almost standing on end. She looked like a blow-dried purple fairy floss.

'Fee-ona,' she shrieked, 'come to my office now.' Whoa, what was going down here? Ster-ewth thought Ozzie, what can Fee possibly have done? He knew she was in a foul mood this morning. She slammed her bedroom door so hard that it nearly fell off its hinges. ('Unhinged', now that's a great word to describe her he thought). That meant if IRK went her she would really give it back. He shuddered.

'Now then my sweet girlie,' IRK began, 'I need your help.' Fee swallowed hard in shock. 'I have more problems than I can count on both hands. Look at all this work here,' she said, pointing to huge piles of paper stacked on the desk. 'And I have so many teachers on stress leave. Have you got some interesting things Granny has taught you that you could teach the classes tomorrow?'

'Well, Ozzie has the report he wrote on Australia. It's called *What Tourists Need to Know About Australia*. I promise you it's good. Pete and I could help him present it.'

'It sounds perfect,' IRK said. Frankly she couldn't have cared if they gave a lesson on how to cut toenails. She just needed time to herself.

Next day, the lesson began with the latest Breakfast Quiz.

'Of course, *I* know *all* the answers,' Fee bragged.

'Drop off your perch.' Samantha was getting panicky now she had *serious* competition for the first time ever.

THE BREAKFAST QUIZ: THE WORLD
THIS IS YOUR PLANET

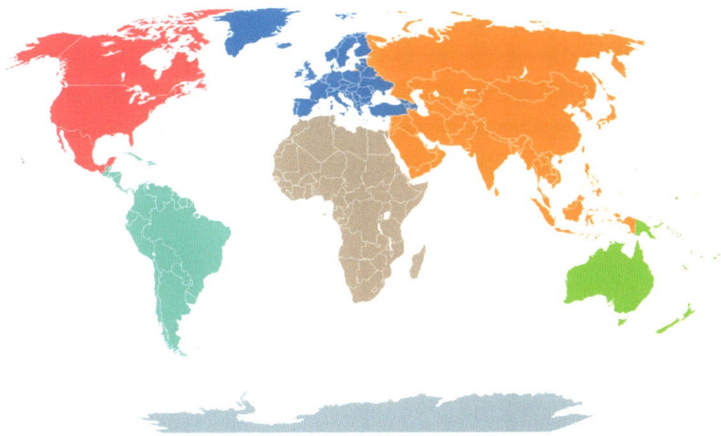

• The other six continents are: Europe, Asia, Africa, North America, South America and Antarctica. The three main oceans are the Atlantic, Pacific and Indian. Can you locate them on the map? Or don't you know one side of the world from the other? If you need help, use the website <maps.com> and play the Geographic Continent Map Game. Or go to Geo Games: Build Planet Earth at <education.nationalgeographic.com>.

• Australia is the world's 6th biggest country. The five countries that are larger are: China, USA, Russia, Brazil and Canada. Can you identify which is which from map outlines below? The colours and patterns on the maps represent each country's national flag.

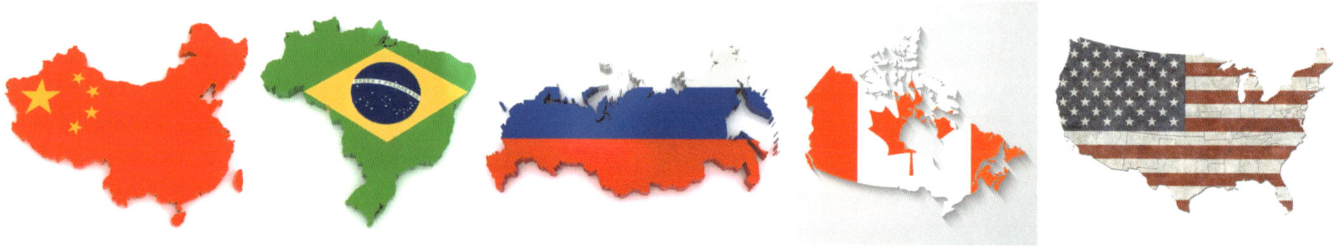

Flag maps of the world's five biggest countries

- In which continent is each of these countries?
- Rank the countries in order of their size starting with the largest.
- Which of them would you visit to see the following: a panda bear, the mighty Amazon rainforest, Disneyland, the city of Moscow, a polar bear?
- Name eight of the world's ten countries whose name begins with the letter 'A'. Here are the jumbled names of a few to help with their first three letters: Algiaer (Africa), Afghananist and Armiane (Western Asia), Albiana, Ausiatr and Androra (Europe).

WHAT'S ON A FLAG?

Flag maps of countries whose name begins with the letter 'A'

- Use an atlas to identify the three countries from their map outlines above. One is in the middle of Europe and is one of the world's forty-eight **landlocked** countries. That means it is entirely surrounded by other countries and doesn't have a coastline. The three flag colours are based on the coat of arms of a ruling family in the 1200s.

One in Africa is the home of the dreadlocks hairstyle. Many of its people have been killed in conflicts or wars and the red part of the flag represents their blood. Black represents the dark-skinned people, and the cogwheel represents industry.

The third is in South America. Rich in silver, its name comes from the Latin word for silver, 'argentum'. Its people wanted freedom from Spain who ruled it. The leader of the revolt against the Spanish chose the flag colours. They represent white clouds parting to reveal blue sky, as is said to have happened when the revolt began. This was seen as a sign of the coming freedom.

COMBINED FROGSVILLE SCHOOL SCORE: 15/40 **YOUR SCORE: /40**

EXTRA ACTIVITIES

If you are interested in flags you might like to find out the background to what is on the flags of the world's five biggest countries.

The website <sciencekids.co.nz/sciencefacts/countries> has fun Country and Flag quizzes, a Capital City quiz and a video on how the world's oceans were formed. It also has games to play. A Google search will find more websites with fun activities about the world.

TRAINING YOUR BRAIN AND MEMORY

Well now, so many things to remember eh? On the above website are memory and brain training exercises. Fee had already gotten into this. You can select aspects of your memory that you would like to improve. Your brain can be trained to remember patterns and locations and to keep track of all the info stored in it. Also skills in recalling info and problem solving can be developed. Daily workout exercises can increase your memory, attention and speed of recall.

Imagine what a whizz-bang know-it-all you could become!

OZZIE'S REPORT

Ozzie began the lesson. He had even washed and combed his hair. He looks one quarter of the way to being a human Fee thought.

'A long time ago, someone turned off the big water tap that sits in the sky above Australia. So, apart from Antarctica, Australia is the world's driest continent. Two thirds of the country is desert or **semi-arid** (near-desert).'

'Someone also damaged the air conditioner over Australia and no one has ever been able to fix it! Now have youse got any idea how hot it can get? The highest recorded temperature is 51.1°C at Cloncurry in Queensland. But at Marble Bar in Western Australia the temperature was over 38°C for 160 days in a row! Ya don't need an oven to cook dinner; ya can fry it on a rock! Truly! Also any visitors goin' out in the bush better take lotsa drinking water. Else they might find themselves in a situation like this lizard or die of thirst in the desert.'

'Don't worry about bringing a towel – there's no water for showers. And tourists better bring lots of toilet paper too because we don't have any in Australia!' Pete said. The class was in uproar once more.

Water shortage is one of Australia's greatest problems

'Speaking of toilets, in Oz (the nickname for Australia), we call a toilet a 'loo' or 'dunny'. Now for a bit of dunny history. In remote places especially where water is scarce, the dunnies are known as 'long drops'. They are benches with a hole in the middle to sit on and a pit underneath. They usually come with red back spiders. Much smaller than a fingernail, one nip and you're a goner. Long drops were once a way of life. Now would you believe they are a major tourist attraction! It's true! Tourists can find examples of great long drops to visit on the Internet. Of course if you don't fancy that you can phone Lulu's Toilet Hire!'

'We even found this article from the Brisbane Courier Mail, dated December 29, 2012.'

WOMAN, 65, TRAPPED AFTER FALLING DOWN LONG DROP TOILET

A woman was climbing off a trailer when she fell backwards into a long drop. She spent a number of hours there before her husband found her.

She suffered a fractured leg but is now in a stable condition in hospital.

Nothing will save you from Australian flies

'Now if you're gonna go walkin' around, there's something *really* important to know. On the world list of the top twenty **venomous** or poisonous snakes, the Indian Cobra is 11th and the King Cobra 16th. But here's the shocking part: all the rest are Australian! Number One is the Inland Taipan that often lives in the burrows of its main prey, the Long-haired Rat. In one bite it can inject more than 40 000 times the venom needed to kill a rat! So visitors had better bring a first aid kit. By the way in Australia we call snakes Joe Blakes.'

'Yeah,' Pete interrupted unable to help himself. 'Not to mention 6 000 species of – guess what? Flies! So buy a fly net but remember to take it off before you eat your scones and cream or blow your nose!'

'Australia has been whacked good and hard by a giant steel frying pan, making it the world's flattest continent. But really, that's because it is the oldest continent, all weather-beaten and broken down by the forces of nature. Ya only got to come here to Frogsville to see the evidence of that – all the old geezers that live here!'

'Once Australia had several mountain ranges as high as the world's highest mountains are now. Old Man Weather has beaten and worn them down. They're just stubs of their former selves. Ya know, just like an old person's teeth. So tourists can leave their mountaineering gear at home. That's not quite true really cause we do we have beautiful mountains like the Snowy Mountains in NSW and Victoria.'

The Snowy Mountains

'Speaking of age, Australia's Aboriginal peoples are the world's longest surviving nation. They have lived here for over 60 000 years, outliving many cultures and even huge empires like the famous Roman Empire. Their rock paintings are the world's oldest. Ancient Aboriginal trading routes are the world's oldest communication lines.'

This famous rock painting of Lightning Man, an Aboriginal creation ancestor, is in Kakadu National Park. He is responsible for the violent lightning storms that occur in Northern Australia as summer approaches. The white band linking his head to his feet is a lightning bolt. He carries a hammer and each time he strikes it on the ground, a storm begins.

'Now before I continue, I'd like to bet that none of youse even know what the gear on the Aussie flag is. Do ya?' A sea of blank faces stared back. 'I bet youse don't even know that we have an Aboriginal flag.' More blank faces told him the answer.

THE AUSTRALIAN FLAG

The Australian Flag was first flown in 1901. The colonies of New South Wales, Western Australia, South Australia, Queensland, Victoria and Tasmania united then to form the Commonwealth of Australia. In the top left corner is the Union Jack or flag of the United Kingdom (England, Scotland, Wales and Northern Ireland). This recognises that the colonies had been ruled by the United Kingdom up until then.

The large seven-pointed star is the Star of the Commonwealth. Six of the points represent the states. The seventh represents the Northern Territory and other territories. The other stars make up the famous group of stars or **constellation** known as the Southern Cross.

THE ABORIGINAL FLAG

The Aboriginal flag is a symbol of **unity** or 'oneness' and national identity for the Aboriginal peoples. It was first flown in 1971. Black represents the people. The yellow is the sun, the giver of life and protector. Red stands for the earth and the spiritual relationship of the people to the land.

WE DO THINGS BIG IN AUSTRALIA!

'Australia is the only continent that is occupied by one country. Dozens of countries make up the others. Even though it is the world's second smallest continent, it is still a big place. Dya know that many cattle stations are bigger than some countries? For example, Anna Creek Station on the edge of the Simpson Desert is bigger than Wales or Israel. It can be a 100 km drive from the homestead to the letterbox! A toothache might see a 600 km drive.'

Uluru measures a whopping 9.4 km around its base.

Ozzie kept glancing at Samantha. Was she impressed? She appeared to be totally bored. In fact she was totally turned off by Ozzie's crude way of talking. The only person she looked at the entire time was the most handsome boy in the class. Ozzie plodded on, feeling very flat.

'Uluru (Ayers Rock) is a major landmark and Australian **icon** or symbol. Famous around the world, it is a sacred

Aboriginal site and is on the **World Heritage List** or list of the most special places. It rises 348 m above the surrounding plain. Once it sat in a sea and it is actually made of sand compressed into hard rock layers. Amazingly, there is more of the rock underground than above ground. If you want to see how far, prepare for a dig of at least 2 500 m!'

'The Great Barrier Reef is the world's largest living structure and coral reef. To see it all you'd need to snorkel over 2 000 km! Not to mention that it's made up of over 2 500 separate reefs! Heaps of different corals and fish live there. Some are deadly. Box jellyfish and stonefish are the deadliest of their kind in the world. But it's okay if you cover up from head to toe. And really, it's only a problem in some areas in summer. Then of course, the odd sea-going saltwater croc likes to pay a visit to the reef sometimes.'

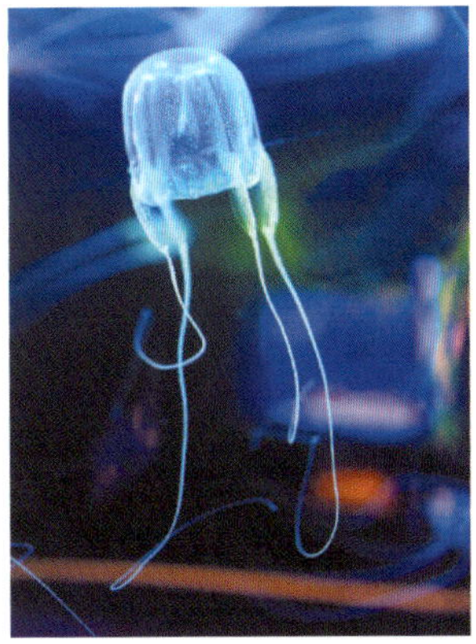

The box jellyfish measures about 20 cm along each side of its box-shaped sides. On each corner of the 'box' are about 15 tentacles. On those tentacles are explosive cells that fire harpoon-shaped **microscopic** or tiny devices that inject the venom.

But none of that's a problem if a tiger shark gets you first! Tiger sharks have twenty-four teeth on both jaws. Each tooth has saw edges. The teeth are razor-sharp and if sharky loses any, others are ready to replace them!

'But don't be put off. The reef has the greatest variety of creatures of any reef in the world. It is truly beautiful.'

Number of species:

- Fish: 1 500
- Hard Corals: 360
- Molluscs (e.g. clams, octopuses, snails): 5 000 or more
- Echinoderms (e.g. star fish, sea urchins): 600
- Sea Snakes: 30
- Whales and dolphins: 30
- Shorebirds: 32

'Why don't you come and explore our fantastic rain forests? You can give a free donation to the Leech Blood Bank. No worries – they'll only suck a bit of blood. You'll know when they're done. When they're nice and swollen up with your blood, they'll drop off. Easy-peasy eh? Then of course, some spiders are so big that they can eat a bird!'

The Nullarbor Plain

The Nullarbor Plain in the southern Australian desert is the one of the world's biggest single limestone deposits. It is an old sea floor that has been lifted up. Its name means 'no trees'. The world's longest underwater cave passage is there in Cocklebiddy Cave. So too, is the world's longest straight stretch of road. Known as The Ninety Mile Stretch it is 147 km long. The world's longest stretch of straight railway line is there too. It is 478 km long.

'In summary, Oz is very special. It has many unique places. I'll tell you about its unusual and fascinating wildlife another time.'

Everyone loved Ozzie's report. Hey maybe this boy wasn't so bad. And his talk was so much fun.

'Thanks pal, I don't like to admit it but I learnt heaps,' Carrot-Hair said. 'But you should make sure tourists know they would be highly unlikely to encounter any of those dangerous creatures. And tell them that we *will* give them towels and dunny paper. It would scare them witless, if they read this.'

But now *all* the classes went on strike.

'We only want Ozzie to teach us from now on from now,' they said. 'We want more, more.' IRK's work in getting back to grammar and algebra were harder than setting a world pole vault record.

Still, Ozzie went home that afternoon full of despair. Samantha had not looked at him, not even once. But little did the kids know what lay in store the following night and the chain of events it would unleash. It would change their lives – *forever.*

THE BREAKFAST QUIZ: AUSTRALIA PART 2

UNJUMBLE OUR NAMES

- Two oceans surrounding Australia: Ficapci (I separate Australia from South America); Nidnia (I separate Australia from Africa and Asia).
- Four seas surrounding Australia: Morti, Amasnt, Lorca, Fauarra.

FIND OUR NAMES

- Two straits or narrow stretches of water: one separating Tasmania from the mainland, the other Australia from New Guinea.

WHAT AM I?

Match these names to these features below: Carpentaria, Great Australian, York.

- A huge **bight** or curve in the coastline of South Australia and Western Australia.
- The largest **cape** or point of land that juts into the sea. I am found at the top of Queensland.
- The next-door neighbour of the above – the largest **gulf** or inlet of the sea.

WHICH WORLD HERITAGE AREAS ARE THESE?

- A large national park east of Darwin. Known for its huge variety of wildlife and Aboriginal rock art sites.
- The world's largest sand island off the coast of Queensland from the town of Hervey Bay.
- A bay in Western Australia named after a large fish and famous for its marine life. The nearest town is Carnarvon.
- A wilderness or **wild** area in Tasmania, especially famous for its very old forests.

COMBINED FROGSVILLE SCHOOL SCORE: 8/15 **YOUR SCORE**: /15

CHAPTER 4: A NIGHTMARE UNFOLDS

A GRUESOME CREATURE IS UNCOVERED

'Right kids, put your boots on,' Granny said one night. 'It's well beyond time for our frog hunt.' Ozzie bolted for his room.

The peace and quiet of frog land was about to be utterly shattered

'Come out of that disgraceful rat-hole,' Fee said, poking her head in Ozzie's doorway. 'If I've got to go on this wretched hunt, then so have you. Pooh it stinks in here! Your bed is the closest thing to a rat's nest I've ever seen.' *Little* did she know as it turned out months later. A cheese sandwich streaked green sat at the back of his desk. Sweaty-smelling clothes and mouldy towels hung off the bed end.

'What is that vile decomposing thing that looks like a fossil poo and smells like one of those stinkhorn fungus things?'

'I dunno,' Ozzie said. 'One of Granny's piglets was in here a while back.'

'Yeah, it looks like the whole tribe of them have been in here. Clean it up before the rest of us catch swine flu.'

'Aw, ya have to *kiss* a pig to catch that. Besides which that disease is easily cured with oinkment.'

'You're *so* primitive. Now come on.'

'Sshh, what's that noise?' Pete whispered, finger up to his lips as the family stepped onto the veranda at 8 pm. 'Listen – brr...brr...brr. It's like the telephone dial tone.'

'*No*,' Granny said, a desperate tone in her voice. 'It can't be. Not here.'

'What?'

'No time for questions,' she shrieked, shooting off like an Olympic sprinter. 'Quick, lock up Phant and Derwent. Find a bucket.' She returned with gloves and a plastic bag. 'We have a monumental disaster here kids. Listen again for the noise. I think it's coming from Phant's food bowl.' She shone her torch. There they were – three foul-looking creatures happily feeding on Chum.

'You are face to face with killers kids. See the horrible-looking gland on the their shoulders? Those glands contain poison. Squeeze them and the poison can shoot as far as a metre. Who will sneak up with me? We'll plonk a bucket over them. Then I'll put my hand under and grab them in this bag.' Ozzie insisted he was the best one to help. Granny should have known better.

Bang, down went the bucket. Granny reached under just as Ozzie squatted down. He toppled, knocking over the bucket. The creatures took off in giant jumps. Brr…brr.

'You clod poll,' Fee screeched. 'What if those hideous things get inside? What'll we do now?' Granny bolted inside putting through a call to her friend, a national park ranger.

'We've got a catastrophe here,' she wailed, explaining the situation. 'Yes, I know you've worked hard to keep this menace off the North Coast. No, I've got no idea how they got here. What worries me is what if any of them mate? With all the eggs they produce we'll have a nightmare on our hands. Okay, see you before dark tomorrow then.'

'What on earth is going on?' Pete asked.

'Don't ask. Let's just get on with the frog hunt.' At that moment Granny really *did* want to send Ozzie to Siberia.

OFF ON THE FROG HUNT

The family picked their way by torchlight down the steep, uneven cow path in the moonless night. Milkshake and Upside Down mooed gently. The sweet, earthy smell of their dung wafted through the steamy air.

'What a witless idea this is,' Fee whispered. 'Pobblebonks and Maniacal Cackle frogs, I mean really! Granny is crackers.'

Pete tripped, landing in a freshly deposited cowpat. Its sloppy mess squished all over his thongs and between his toes.

'Ho, you've just had a Close Encounter of the Turd Kind,' Ozzie laughed. 'Don't ya just love that smell of cow dung? I reckon it's one of the greatest smells on earth.'

'Well we all know where your taste is,' Fee snapped. 'I won't mention the word – it's too unrefined. As for you Pete, you'll probably get foot and mouth disease now.'

As the family climbed the path through the towering trees, night wrapped a coal-black coat around them. Weird shadows jumped out from the trees. And then – a blood-curdling scream pierced the air. Three shivering, terrified children grabbed onto Granny.

'It's okay. It's only a barking owl. That's the noise it makes when hunting. And it's a privilege to hear it, because animals are so rare up here. See, you think I'm a crackpot for living out here. But I bought this place to protect the forest and its creatures. Mine is one of the few forest patches left here.'

WAS OZZIE LOSING HIS MIND?

'Hey it's like a fantasy land eh?' Ozzie enthused as they reached the rain forest. He shone his torch on the mass of thick, twisted vines looping up the trees like giant hoops. Flying foxes screeched, fighting over palm fruits.

'Have you got maggots in your head?' Fee asked. 'Are you trying to tell us that for once you're enjoying being off your bum?'

'See these magic toadstools and mushrooms, all shapes, sizes and colours of the rainbow?' Ozzie asked. He was enchanted.

'I'm lovin' every minute of this. It's another world, far more excitin' than watching TV.' Ozzie grinned as his torch shone into the holes where a strangler fig had not yet completely closed over the tree it was slowly squeezing to death. Granny explained that the massive fig started its life as a seed deposited in bird poo high on a branch. The seed **germinates** or sprouts and leaves begin to grow. Then slowly the plant sends roots down and around the tree.

'Well ain't this nature stuff just pure magic?'

GRANNY WASN'T BONKERS AFTER ALL!

'How do we know where to look for the frogs?' Pete asked Granny.

'We must look in the right **habitat** or place the frog is **adapted** or suited to living in. Pobblebonk habitat is swamps, lakes, streams and dams. The Maniacal Cackle Frog is an **arboreal** or tree-dwelling frog. Its habitat is forests, scrub and open areas near water.'

At last the dam with its beautiful mauve water lilies came into view.

'We'll look for the Pobblebonk or Eastern Banjo Frog first. Listen for a noise like a banjo string being plucked. What a racket eh?' The frog songs ranged from deep-throated grunts to tinkling bells. 'They are going berserk because it has been raining,' Granny explained. 'During the day or when it is dry, frogs burrow to stop their skin drying out. They don't drink water, you see. Instead they absorb water through their skin. This means they must keep their skin moist. So they come out at night especially after rain when everything is damp.'

'It is the males making the racket, advertising themselves to the girl frogs. In Froglish they are all saying the same thing.'

Frogs have a **vocal sac**, like a small balloon under the chin. It acts as an **amplifier** that makes their calls louder when filled with air. Gee, just how puffed about himself could a fella be eh?

'Hey Sweetlips, I'm over here, come and kiss me! Don't worry about the mouse I just swallowed, my breath is still sweet.'

Then Pete heard the noise – 'bonk, plonk, bonk'. But where was it coming from? A frog you see, throws its call, fooling you as to where it is.

'How will we pinpoint it in this din?' Pete asked.

'First put these sterile gloves on. Gloves must *always* be worn when touching frogs otherwise we can transmit diseases to them. Stand several metres apart and listen carefully.' Granny counted to five. 'Now shine your torches at the point from which you think a call is coming. Look in the area where our torch beams cross.'

'There he is!' Ozzie said, picking the frog up gently. So Granny wasn't bonkers at all! Well not quite, he thought.

'You mean we came all this way for this,' Fee whinged. 'He's so *ordinary*. Not like those brightly coloured frogs you see in books.'

'Have a closer look – he's quite interesting,' Ozzie said. 'See the warty lumps and the pale yellow stripe between his eye and shoulder? His belly is blotchy white. I guess the muscly legs are for jumping and the short front legs would prop him up when sitting. I reckon he's 6 cm long.'

'Well done,' Granny said. 'The blotchy or **mottled** colours help the frog blend in with his habitat. This protects him from **predators** or creatures that think he's a nice snack.'

'Speaking of blending,' Ozzie said, 'dya know what is red and green and runs round at 100 km an hour? A red-eyed tree frog in a blender! What kind of shoes do frogs wear? Open-toad of course! And when they break a leg they are most unhoppy!'

'Don't put it anywhere near me,' Fee shrieked, jumping back as Ozzie, all revved up, put the frog near her. 'Slimy revolting thing, I'm terrified.'

'Geez, get real. It's just a harmless frog. Here, give it a pat.' So she touched it – lightly.

'Why is he all warty?' she asked, shrinking back. 'And why do his eyes bulge? Is it some awful disease? Can we catch it?'

Pobblebonk Frog

Bumps provide more surface area for absorbing water – they're not warts at all. See how the eyes and nostrils sit high on the head? That is so frogs can see and hear when in the water. Their eyes like a wide-angle camera lens, allow enemies to be spotted. And do you notice the bulging eyes? Frogs have bad table manners. They close their eyes when swallowing something whole. Their eyes sink through holes in the skull to help force food down the throat!

Like many frogs, Pobblebonks sit quietly then suddenly leap out at their prey. They flick out their sticky tongues to lasso insects because they don't have chewing teeth.

SMOKING OUT THE MANIACAL CACKLE FROG

Maniacal Cackle Frog

The kids crept towards the trees. It wasn't long until the high-pitched lengthy cackle 'cra-ah-ah-ah-ahhk' was heard. It really did sound like a maniac crying out. Cupping his ear, Pete tracked it down. It hid under the flaking bark, waiting for some unknowing insect to crawl by. Almost 7.5 cm long, it is one of Australia's largest frogs.

'Wow!' Ozzie said excitedly, turning him over. 'He's got the cutest finger and toe pads. That would be to give him grip for climbing I guess. Isn't this weird – his pupils are cross-shaped. His skin feels smooth as silk. He looks just like a leaf eh? That must be for **camouflage** to disguise him from his enemies. I've never seen anything so cute.'

Could this possibly be my brother – in love with a frog? Fee thought. Is he going to become a nature-tragic?

'Ah yes, but what about the half-webbing between his toes?' Granny added. 'That allows him to parachute through the treetops. And this frog comes in a variety of colours. It can even change colour for different camouflage!'

DESCRIBING A FROG

'Okay now,' Ozzie said, 'let's see if we have it right. To tell frog species apart we need to look at:

- The call
- The shape of the eye pupil
- The colour, especially of the back, sides, belly and inner thighs. Is the colour plain, mottled or marbled?
- Whether the skin is warty or smooth
- Body length
- Whether the fingers and toes have pads and/or webbing.'

Climbing frogs like this Tree Frog have sticky toe pads to give them grip

Frogs that swim and parachute have webbing between the toes. This allows them to move faster.

Can you describe this frog using Ozzie's checklist above? If you were the scientist in charge of giving this frog a name, what would you call it? How would you describe it?

A FROGGY TALE

The next morning found Fee dead asleep in class.

'Wake up girlie and do your sums,' IRK scolded. 'What's the matter with you?'

'We were out all night hunting Pobblebonks and Maniacal Cackle Frogs.'

'Don't tell me such porkies. No such creatures exist. You must have been dreaming.'

'You're wrong.'

'Well prove it to me then.'

Fee related the whole story of the frog hunt.

'You'll never guess what else happened,' she said, all bright-eyed now. 'When we got home, I went for a wee. Something enormous leapt up the toilet bowl. Jumping up like a rocket, I flushed the loo. Up it leapt again. Help, I screamed. Up the hall ran Granny armed with the fire extinguisher and Ozzie with the broom. Something dreadful is in the toilet bowl I howled. It tried to bite my bottom.'

'Ozzie took a peek in the bowl. As if any self-respectin' creature would want to go anywhere near *your* bottom, he said. And you think *you* got a fright? Imagine the fright that poor frog got at the sight of you on the toilet!'

'Well why *would* any self-respecting creature be in a toilet bowl, especially one that *you* have used?'

'It's a 'bog' frog of course, you silly piddock!'

'Don't be so crude!'

'Come on, it's just a green tree frog. Look at his perfect camouflage and his cute toe pads. Come on be brave. *You* fish him out. So I plucked up the courage because I so desperately needed to pee and he was beautiful, truly.'

'Why is he in the toilet bowl I asked?'

'You know, Ozzie reckons the frog even sits on the loo and reads the paper while he's waiting for me!'

'Remember that Granny said frogs need to be moist at all times. That's why they love toilets, tank taps, pot plants and drains.'

'I even carried the frog all the way outside and he gazed up at me with his beautiful eyes. I fell in love – a friend at last. Maybe the only one I'll ever have in this rotten place. But this morning the frog was back in the loo.'

'Look down here on the floor, Ozzie said. Little frog scats or calling cards were everywhere. You'd think with a toilet bowl this big he could at least aim properly!'

'But I don't know what to do. What if we poo on him? Will he drown if we flush the loo? We think we'll have to use the ancient outside dunny.'

'Geez is that why frogs are always in our loo?' Carrot Hair said. 'And fancy us living in Frogsville and not knowing about Pobblebonks.'

'But that's not all,' Fee continued, giving a detailed description of the gruesome creatures they found. 'We've never seen anything so revolting.' Awe-struck, the other kids couldn't wait to tell their parents.

Feeling she had at last got the attention she deserved, Fee started to settle down. She almost became the perfect student. Hmm, old IRK thought things over.

'How about tomorrow you tell us some more of what you learned?'

'This is my big chance,' Fee said at home that night. 'I never would have dreamt that my life would change because of *frogs*! Please help me write a good report and design some interesting activities.'

'Okay as long as I get to do one too,' Pete said. All night the kids pored over Granny's books and Fee made her presentation.

PUMPKIN PATCH POST - FROGS UNDER THE MICROSCOPE

Frogs are **vertebrates** or animals with backbones. They belong to a group of animals called **amphibians** (am-fib-ee-anz). These animals have three stages of development - egg, **larva** (like a grub) and adult. Amphibians also include **newts** and **salamanders** and a weird lot like large earthworms. The big 'A' word is from a Greek word meaning 'double life'. This relates to the different life stages, for example of tadpoles and adult frogs. In water, amphibians breathe through **gills**, those slit-like things most fish have. On land they breathe through lungs.

People who study amphibians are called herpetologists or herps for short!

FROG ESPIONAGE FOR EARTH DETECTIVES - WHERE TO GET THE LOW DOWN

Here is the good info needed to find out which frogs live in your local area and how to identify a frog species:

- Do an Internet search using the name of your country + frog identification, for example 'Australia + frog identification'. Frog calls can be listened to on some websites.
- General information including community activities, surveys and tips on building and looking after frog ponds can be found at the website <frogsaustralia.org au>.
- For info on frog life cycles check out <kiddyhouse.com>. There is also fascinating frog stuff including songs and poems.

FROGGY TRICKS

Assess your herp detective skills.

Strawberry Poison Dart Frog

- From this story can you track down at least twenty-four clever tricks or ways that help frogs to live successfully in their habitats? These are called **adaptations**. An example is mottled skin colours to blend in with the surrounds. Look for adaptations for climbing, jumping, feeding, protection, communication ('talking') and survival.
- How many of these adaptations can you find on the tree frog on page 35 and the Strawberry Poison Dart Frog? Develop a profile of these frogs describing everything that you can, including the colours.
- If you were the scientist in charge of naming the Tree Frog and Strawberry Poison Dart Frog what would you name them?

- The Poison Dart Frog can change its skin into twenty different colours. What do you think the bright red colour might be for? Find out what other colours it can change to.
- How does this frog come by its name?
- Research how frogs change their colour.

WHAT'S IN A NAME?

Find out about these frogs: poison dart frog, shoemaker frog, javelin frog, striped rocket frog, platypus frog, turtle frog, holy cross frog. How do these frogs come by their names - can you tell from their pictures?

IRK WAS GOBSMACKED

IRK had never seen the students so interested. She wasn't there for Ozzie's report on Australia, of course. She was astounded by Fee's report. I have to admit she is bright, she thought. Perhaps the way to settle these new kids down is to give them some limelight. I'll suggest it at the next staff meeting. After all, I'm running out of money for teachers' stress leave.

'That was brilliant,' she said, smiling through gritted teeth. 'But please do remember the word is 'urinate' not 'wee'.'

'I *come* from a brilliant family,' Fee responded. 'My Granny was a geography teacher and she knows *everything* there is to know about the world.'

We'll just see about that, IRK thought.

CHAOS IN FROGSVILLE

That afternoon a fleet of cars arrived at the farm. An angry mob marched up to the house led by Humph, the next-door neighbour. His eyes were like white marble shot with tiny streaks of blood. They bulged just like frogs' eyes. Pete greeted him at the door.

'Geez,' he said, 'do you use your eyes to swallow your food too?'

Humph

Pete reckoned Humph's face looked like it had been bashed in with a shovel. The back of his neck was crinkled with rolls of fat, like the old bulldog down the road. 'Old Bulldog' became Pete's nickname for him.

Humph snorted through his flattened nose, ridged with its dark hairs. Black hairs corkscrewed out his nostrils and ears. Pity some of that hair couldn't be transplanted onto his head Pete thought.

'You stupid woman,' he yelled at Granny, his face flushed devil's-cloak red. Bits of spit flew out his mouth. 'We know all about them bleeding critters that are loose on your farm. They've come down from Queensland in that load of macadamia trees you bought. One of my prize breeding Rhode Island Red hens has eaten one and died.'

'And what will happen to our cats and dogs? I'll hold yer responsible for this nightmare. I'll take yer to court if you don't get this sorted quick smart. I'll get yer back yet. I'll run yer out of town.'

Granny, you see had reported Humph for cutting down a pile of rainforest trees without permission. That is against the law. He was taken to court and fined $10 000.

'I *had* to report him,' Granny explained to the kids later that night. 'Stupid old coot, we'll have no rainforest left, except mine. Every tree that is removed means animals lose their homes and food sources. Most of them die. That is because they can not move into another animal's territory.'

But Humph had another reason for wanting Granny to get the blame. It was a reason that only *he* knew.

Meanwhile, Granny's ranger friend pulled up, 'calm down,' he pleaded to the crowd. 'We'll deal with it. Organise yourselves into search parties. Check their favourite hideouts – pot plants, garden mulch, standing water and dams. Clean up any rubbish where they may shelter in the day. At night they hang around lights that attract insects. So switch on your outside lights.'

Now the pressure was on. In deathly silence, able to hear their own hearts thumping, the kids crept about with Granny every night. She dragged them everywhere. Her temper was something else. You couldn't blame her with everyone phoning all day long. How much longer must we keep our animals locked up? What if those bleeding monsters mate? The village was on edge, everyone arguing. Nobody could find the creatures. But what if Granny in her foul mood decided to send the kids to Siberia? Pete dreamt that she pinned a chart to the kitchen wall.

WILL I SEND THE CHILDREN TO SIBERIA?

POINTS FOR YES: 65 000 POINTS FOR NO: 0

OZZIE'S NIGHTMARES

Was the pressure too much? One night at 4 am a car arrived at The Pumpkin Patch. A policeman hauled Ozzie out of the car, bleary-eyed and staggering with tiredness.

'Madam, your boy is up to no good. I caught him creeping around the village. *I* reckon he was planning to steal stuff. *He* reckons he was sleepwalking. But how could he be?' he said, eyeing him off. Ozzie wore a huge old coat he found in the shed. Its pockets were full of tools. 'And why was he carrying a bucket? Look, he's even got gloves so he doesn't leave fingerprints. I'll be keeping an eye on him I tell you.'

Ozzie insisted he'd been having such nightmares about those creatures that it was causing him to go hunting in his sleep. That week he thumped down the hall at all hours of night, his pyjama bottoms wet with dew.

'Have you been eating Phant's Chum in your sleep too?' Pete accused him. 'Six tins are missing! You're not that hungry are you?'

DESIGNING A FROG POND

'Let's try to get in the good books of Frogsville,' Ozzie said next day. He wanted to take people's attention off his nightly wanderings. 'What if we suggest building a frog pond in the public garden? It would go so beautifully with the village name.' The Mayor thought it was a great idea. Everyone got behind the project. Pete did most of the research and design work.

Frogs were soon heard in the pond. Next a foamy raft of Pobblebonk eggs appeared. The tadpoles or **polliwogs** took 3-25 days to develop, breathing through gills. Six weeks later back legs grew, then front. But where had the tails gone? At this stage, the tadpoles absorbed their own tails! Lungs developed and mouths widened. They ate **algae** or small plant life.

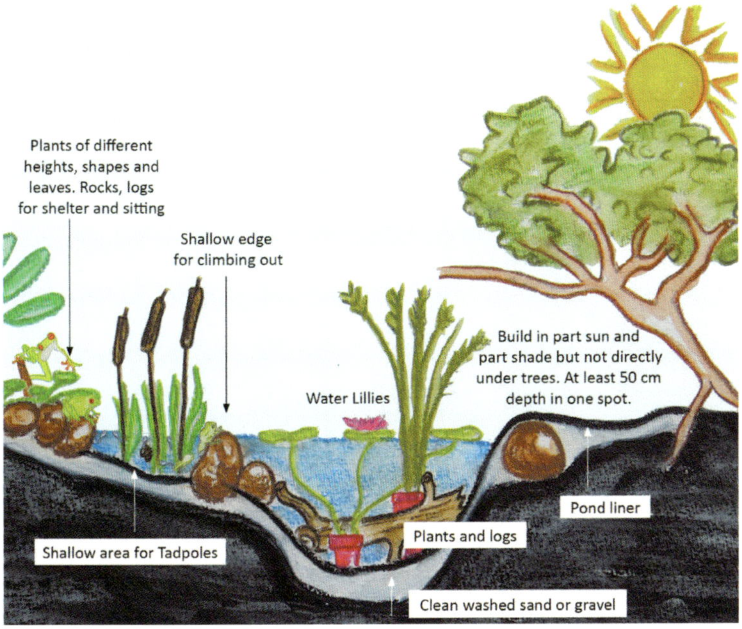

Pete's design sketch of the frog pond

About three and a half months after hatching, the tadpoles became young frogs or **froglets**. These changes have a big mouthful of a name – **metamorphosis**. Same thing as when a grub changes into a moth. Now they ate insects and spent most of the time on land. An adult frog that can live on land or water is the final outcome of this amazing process.

Old IRK allowed the students to go to the pond to study **food webs** or the feeding relationships between plants and animals in a habitat. Pete produced a report about frogs' eggs that won him admiration. Things were looking up.

FROG LIFE CYCLE

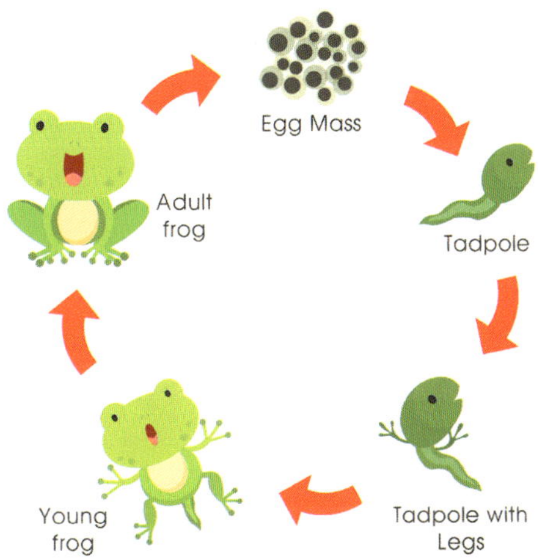

A SIMPLE FROGGY FOOD WEB

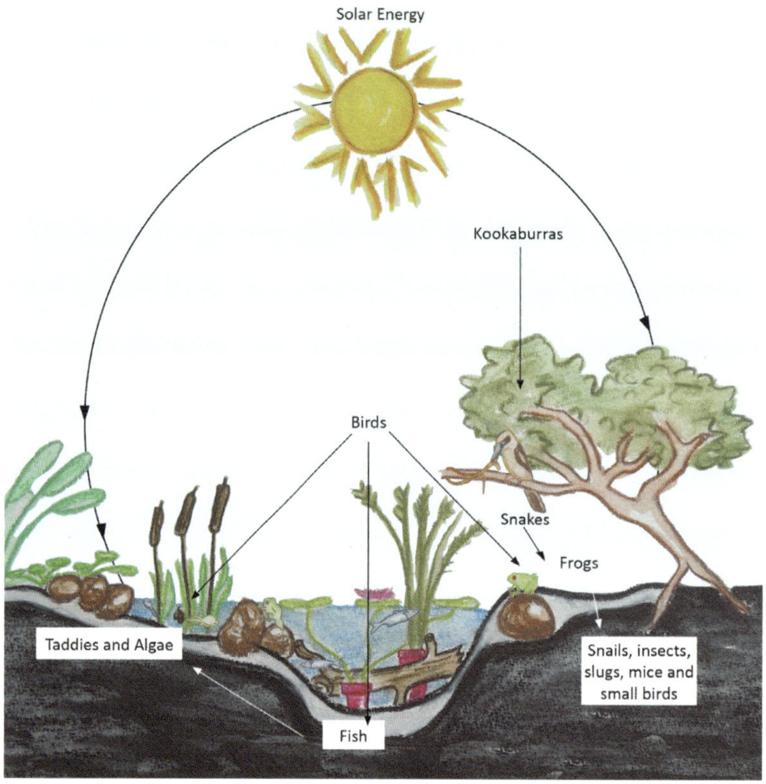

PUMPKIN PATCH POST – AMAZING THINGS ABOUT FROGS' EGGS

An example of frog spawn

A Pobblebonk lays 50 000 eggs in the ten years of her reproductive life. She uses her front legs like an eggbeater, whipping up clear jelly and bubbles. This foamy raft keeps the eggs at the surface where the water is warmest. The female may even carry that lazy boy-frog to the egg-laying place on her back. After laying the eggs, the male releases his sperm over them. This is called **fertilisation**. Clumped together and covered in a ball of protective jelly, the eggs are called **spawn**.

HOW DO FROGS PROTECT THEIR EGGS?

- The Red-eyed Tree Frog sticks her eggs to the underside of leaves that fall into the water when the tadpoles hatch.
- The Darwin's Frog protects the eggs in his vocal sac - bet that stops him advertising himself to the girls!
- Female Gastric Brooding Frogs give birth to the eggs out of their mouths! They are the world's only creatures to do this. Their stomach chemistry changes and they do not eat. The tadpoles feed from the remains of yolk stored in their bodies. Found only in a small area of Queensland, the two species of this frog are rarely seen now.
- The Marsupial Frog carries the tadpoles in slit-like pouches. He sits in the middle of the eggs just before hatching occurs and the tadpoles jump into the pouch. Weeks later, he helps the froglets out by opening the pouches with his hind toe.
- The male Midwife Toad carries the eggs wound around his hind legs.

SOMETHING WENT THUMP IN THE NIGHT

While the frog pond was a roaring success, not one of those wretched creatures was caught yet. (Smart Australian kids will have worked out that the menace was the dreaded cane toad). The kids went to bed full of anxiety once more. The old house seemed to creak and groan more than ever that night. Then at 3 am they were woken by a thunderous thud on the veranda.

'Do you think it's a village lynching party? Ya know – come to capture and hang us,' Ozzie whispered as they crept out.

'Your knocking knees sound like castanets in a percussion band,' Fee said to Pete. But there at the front door was a brown satchel with a bright blue button. What was it? How on earth did it get there? And what was in it?

CHAPTER 5: THE BIRTH OF THE POBBLEBONK EARTH DETECTIVE CLUB

THE SATCHEL

'Do you think Humph has dropped a bomb on us?' Pete whispered.

Bravely, Fee picked up the satchel. She couldn't hear any ticking. Opening it with shaking hands, she found a letter on bright blue paper.

The Sherlock Holmes International
Detective School (SHIDS)
221 Baker St, London
1100 hrs March 1st

Dear Children,

It has come to my attention that you are intending to form an Earth Detective Club. You *must* undertake training with our school first. You will receive our correspondence in brown satchels. When you need to make contact, place your message in a satchel. Press its blue button and hang it on the veranda.

Detectives must develop many skills. If you pass all tests then you will be given official detective status. For the time being you are on probation. Being the oldest, Ozzie and Fee will have the role of Senior Detective. Pete will have the rank of Junior Detective. The Phantom will play the role of Chief Sniffer Dog.

To qualify for permanent membership of our esteemed organisation you must:

- Behave in a manner which sets an example to others especially non-detectives or Earth Ignoramuses as we call them.
- Choose a uniform and wear it proudly along with your name tag stating your rank.
- Undertake the tasks we set.
- Keep thorough case notes. These will be filed and used by other detectives.

And please remember, we are watching you. We will see and know everything you do. That includes how many lemon tarts you eat Ozzie!

Yours sincerely,
Horace A. Fitzwilliam
Principal

THE BIRTH OF THE CLUB

'Who on earth is Sherlock Holmes?' Pete asked, as he proudly flexed his biceps. They had grown a *whole* centimetre since Granny had him doing weights every day.

Sherlock Holmes

'He was the world's greatest ever detective,' Fee replied. 'Beginning his career in 1887 in London, he was a master of disguise, reasoning and forensic science. You know, it was him we watched in that horror film, *The Hound of the Baskervilles*.'

'Someone must be playing a joke surely,' Pete said. 'Or maybe Granny put the satchel there?'

'Dunno, but I think we'd better give it a shot,' Ozzie replied. 'Otherwise our club might be at risk.'

You see, what happened after that first frog hunt as the kids sat drinking cocoa at the kitchen table was this.

'Wow, I'm just blown away,' Ozzie bubbled. 'I had no idea frogs were so interesting. There could be a billion fascinating things to explore here. Why don't we form an Earth Detective Club and get stuck into it? Ya know we could get into spiders, leeches, bats, Granny's wildlife poo and animal tracking thing, the whole bit. At least we'd have something to *do*. Let's face it, we're never gonna have our old life back.'

Pete jumped around, 'hey we could call it the Bobbleponk Earth Detective Club. We could even use that old artist's studio out the back for our office. It would be perfect. You know, well away from any prying eyes.'

'Can we buy some gear?' Pete begged Granny, handing her a written list. On it was these items: periscopes, test tubs, scalps, spacemen jars, books, fling cabinets and desks.

'Well, I suggest you start with a dictionary and spelling book, young man.' But Granny's eyes had lit up. Maybe she was starting to get somewhere. She gazed at the photos on the wall. Memories flooded back again – of climbing volcanoes in Bali, walking on glaciers in Alaska and hot air ballooning over Turkey.

'What better way to spend my uncle's inheritance?' she said. 'Yes we'll set up an office. Then how about I map out some interesting places and we go exploring?'

Granny kitted up to go *inside* an extinct volcano

'Aw geez I dunno,' Ozzie drawled. 'I could buy 5 000 Mars Bars, 10 000 lemon tarts and fifty cases of Spam in a Can with that money.'

Granny rang the children's mother and discussed her plan, 'I'll keep them busy. Give them fun and adventure like I've had. I'll find challenging situations to shift them out of their comfort zone. It will improve Pete's confidence, Fee's foul moods and Ozzie's self-esteem.'

'What's self-steam?' Pete asked, overhearing.

'Self-esteem. It means having a healthy opinion of yourself.'

And so Granny's *Grand Plan for the Mathieson Children* was born.

THE POBBLEBONK DETECTIVE CLUB BECAME OFFICIAL

The office was completed in two weeks. It was every kid's dream. A coat of blue paint covered the old iron roof and walls. A new set of steps set it off.

'The secret password will be *Polliwog*,' Pete said. 'No one will know what it means so it will keep unwelcome visitors out.' He put up a sign again with his poor spelling.

Bobbleponk Earth Dective Club   Secret Kids Busyness

Visitors by A-Point-Ment Only   Trespatchers Will Be Execooted

ADULTS FOR-BIDDEN   FEES NE-GOAT-IBLE

Granny designed the office to double as living quarters for the kids. Ah, she thought taking a deep breath – peace and quiet for me at last! The detectives had everything they needed. They could crash out when cases took them late into the night, not to mention holding top-secret meetings. The office veranda with its panoramic views was an ideal spot for nature watching.

Fee got the low down on how to set up a website and Facebook page. The children got busy.

'We should put something there about Granny,' Ozzie said.

'I've got a *great* idea,' Pete replied, outlining his thoughts.

'Whoa,' Ozzie laughed, 'I think that's just beautiful! Can we do it dya think?'

Well do it they did. And later when Granny found out, she was close to booking three airfares to Siberia.

On the new shelves, Pete organised the books on bats, snakes, animal tracks and a mountain of others that they bought.

Ozzie opened a book called *Australian Backyard Naturalist* by Peter Macinnis, published by the National Library of Australia.

'Wow!' he said. 'This is every Earth Detective's dream. Look at the all this wonderful stuff on ants, spiders, bees and a pile of other things. And look at all the interesting projects in it that we could do. It's even won an award from the state Premier. Granny was right. Bees and things *are* fascinating.' He spent the rest of the day poring over the book, not even stopping for a choco-date.

'Look, I might have fallen in love with a frog, but you can forget me getting involved in any of those horrible things!' Fee said. Little did she know what was in store.

That night she made pancakes and cocoa and they designed a Breakfast Quiz. Fee wanted to make it as hard as possible so Samantha would fail. This quiz challenge can be found at the end of the chapter.

Snuggling down in the comfy bunks the kids had no worries about using the outside dunny with its red-back spiders. They had their own! It was all so cosy until half way through the night when Ozzie let rip.

'You nearly blew the roof off,' Fee laughed.

'Aw, you do exaggerate so.'

'It's true. I felt it vibrate!' Then crash went something on the roof. That definitely was *not* Ozzie.

'Oh no,' Pete said. 'Do you think it's another one of those satchels? How would Horace Fitzwilliam know we're out here now? It *must* be Granny doing this.'

MEMORANDUM

DATE: 0300 hrs March 17th **SUBJECT:** Get on the case fast!

Get on the case *now.* I'm setting your first tasks as frog scientists or herps. You must pass Certificate 1 in Frog Science. First get out there and catch those gruesome creatures that you seem to have forgotten about. Next you have some deaths to investigate as set out in the attached brief. And start educating your village more about frogs and toads. After all you do live in *Frogsville!*

Horace A. Fitzwilliam

THE INVESTIGATION

- Find out how to identify a cane toad.
- Learn the differences between frogs and toads.
- Find out why cane toads are such a problem.
- Locate the two dead bodies in the Frogsville Garden near the War Memorial. See to it that an autopsy is carried out and a cause of death established. Then *take action.*
- Check out what is now in your frog pond and do something about it - fast.
- Research why frogs are in so much trouble.
- Then hold a meeting and tell the residents of Frogsville they must pull their socks up. Explain how they can give frogs a helping hand.

AN OFFICIAL MURDER INVESTIGATION

'I've just been up to the frog pond,' a weary Ozzie said as he staggered into breakfast next morning. He was weary not just from the effort but because he had been awake worrying about the toads for hours each night. Ideas for snaffling Samantha buzzed around his head too. But Ozzie did not have the courage to act on them.

'I found something and I have a dreadful feeling it could be the end of Granny. I want to check it out under the cover of darkness tonight while we look for the bodies.'

'Now that we're on an official murder investigation, we must wear our uniforms. Make sure you pull your hat brims down for disguise,' Ozzie whispered as they got ready. 'Come on, Sherlock would never have gone out without his hat,' he said as Fee complained bitterly. Ozzie chose the uniforms. She thought it was another idea from his *Theatre of the Ridiculous*. Stuffing detective gear in the pockets of their trench coats, the kids crept over the creaky floorboards. It was 11 pm as they climbed out of the bedroom window.

The Chief Sniffer Dog had the honour of the lead position, alerting the kids every time he picked up a sound. The kids crept along, ducking into bushes and ditches whenever a car was heard. Pete wiped the sweat from his brow. The pressure was really on. Humph had complained to the Ministry of the Environment. He wanted Granny trapped and disposed of. At last they made it to the village garden, edging their way between the flowerbeds and hedges. Ozzie shone his torch into the pond.

'See the string of small dark spots: they're cane toad eggs all right. So they *have* mated! What a catastrophe! This must be kept secret. If we don't protect Granny we'll end up back in the city. And that will be the end of all our adventures.' The eggs were scooped out and laid on the cement pathway to dry. That is the best way to kill them.

'Are you sure they're cane toad eggs? We wouldn't want to harm native frogs.'

'Yep, I'm sure all right.'

Cane toad eggs are 3 mm thick chains of black eggs each about 1 mm thick with a gooey gelatine coating around them. 'Toadpoles' are easy to identify: they are pure and dark black. They group into a large slow-moving mass at the water's edge. Unlike native tadpoles they often don't surface to breathe. A cane toad can lay 30 000 eggs in just one sitting! No wonder they've spread so far around the country! The eggs are poisonous and 'toadpoles' eat native tadpoles.

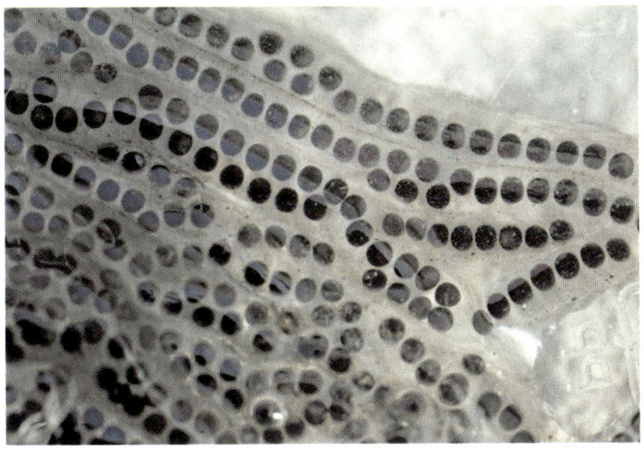

Native frogs lay a frothy mass of eggs without the jelly-like strands of the cane toad. Native tadpoles are usually dark too. But their lighter-coloured 'belly skin' is **transparent** – you can see through it.

Fee battled to keep her torchlight steady, her heart hammering with fear. She had no idea what awful thing they might find as they began searching for the bodies. What on earth would they be? Pete sealed off a ten metre square area with his crime scene tape. Fee was down on all fours when Ozzie sounded the alarm.

'Quick, turn off your torches and hide. People are leaving the hall from the Rhode Island Red Hen Owners' Ball.' Racing behind the War Memorial, they froze. But overdosed on Brussels sprouts, Ozzie was having trouble holding in his wind. He let rip with a you-know-what that thundered through the night. Suddenly a huge beam of light shone down.

'What the hell are youse doing?' Humph demanded.

'Why are you dressed in that ridiculous gear you loony tunes?' The cranky Old Bulldog's thick eyebrows, knitted in purl and plain arched right up his forehead. The purple veins on his temples pulsed angrily.

He seemed to haunt the kids, determined to make their lives hell. A policeman with huge feet was with him. How can we possibly explain our way out of this Fee thought, rigid with fear?

'We've been instructed by Sherlock Holmes to look for two dead bodies,' Pete said.

'Do you have a fever boy? Sherlock exists only in fiction.'

'Actually, we're constructing a scene for a murder play I'm writing,' Ozzie said. Unable to help himself he let rip again nearly blowing his trousers off. Staggering backwards Humph and the policeman pinched their nostrils in disbelief.

'Do you think it's something the Old Girl feeds them?' Big Foot asked Humph. 'How else could they be such cabbage heads? And produce gas like that in the process?'

'No I think it's in their genes. You know the Old Girl is crackers. She even carries on about loving trees.'

'Geez, who needs enemas when we can have friends like you?' Pete complained. Giggling, Fee dug him in the ribs and whispered.

'The word is enemies. An enema is what Granny uses for her constipation!'

Pete pictured himself in prison and a shudder ripped through his body.

'I just don't believe you kids are for real,' Big Foot said.

'We're for real all right,' Ozzie said. 'And don't give us any grief pal. I'm a Senior Detective. I outrank you.'

'Right, that's it. I'm arresting you for impersonating an officer, amongst other charges.' He opened the pad he was carrying. Pete saw the heading on the page: Arrest Warrant.

Humph took the policeman aside, 'I'd think twice about that,' he warned. 'The big one there will stink out your police station. And without doubt, they'll cause *endless* trouble.'

'We know you're angry about being deported from Sydney,' the policeman snapped. 'No wonder you were sent away. Why they didn't bung you in a lunatic asylum is beyond me. You've done nothing but wreak havoc ever since you got here.'

Rivers of tears streamed down Pete's face.

'Oh please,' he begged. 'We just lost our Dad and we've been separated from our Mum.' Big Foot felt a tiny twinge of sympathy. He gave in and rang Granny.

'Do you know what your deranged grandkids are up to? One more strike and I'll put them in juvenile detention.'

What could Granny say though, when the kids reported that they were on official SHIDS business?

THE DREADED CANE TOAD

But meanwhile, why was Frogsville so up in arms over the toads? The cane toad you see, was **introduced** into Australia or brought from another country. The idea was that it would eat insect pests in Queensland's sugar cane fields. But the toads weren't too interested in that. They moved out to more exciting real estate where they developed a liking for other tasty morsels including the eggs of native frogs.

Not only that but thousands of creatures die every day from eating cane toads, because of the poison in their glands. Also, when species like toads are introduced, everything gets out of balance. Every type or **species** of plant and animal in an environment plays a role including providing food for other species. All of this has evolved over millions of years and is finely balanced. It's like this with the cane toad:

EFFECTS OF CANE TOADS ON NATIVE ANIMALS

TOADS EAT:

- Insects that play useful roles
- Native frogs, small reptiles and mammals, and birds
- Up to 200 'food items' each night!

TOADS ARE EATEN BY:

- Birds, reptiles, small mammals

TOADS COMPETE WITH:

- Native animals for food and habitat

TOADS ARE POISONOUS TO:

- Toads and their eggs are poisonous to everything that eats them

'Did you know that cane toads are training for the long jump and the foot races at the Olympic Games?' Ozzie asked. 'The ones up north take steroids to develop longer, stronger arms and legs. They train by moving further and faster across the country. The head of the toad empire has put up signs.'

GO WEST YOUNG TOADS
FOLLOW THE HIGHWAYS TO RICH REAL ESTATE
RESTAURANTS GALORE, FOOD LAID ON
GREAT SWIMMING HOLES AND PLACES TO RELAX

'It's true!' Ozzie insisted. 'Those smart little devils have even learned to use the highways to head west. It makes their journey faster. Since 1935 they have moved 2 600 km across the country. Mating is another thing they train hard at, increasing from a population of 100 or so when they were brought here to 1.5 billion now!'

PORTRAIT OF THE KILLER

The toad's scientific name is *Bufo marinus*. No wonder it's poisonous with a name like that! And get a look at that face! How could you ever forget it?

'Bufo, that's now my fave word,' Ozzie laughed.

The features that most set the toad apart from native frogs are the poison gland, the ear- drum and the bony ridge. Can you see them? The cane toad usually measures 100-150 mm long and can weigh up to 1 kg. Cane toads often gather in groups under outside lights to catch insects. The call is a trill that comes from the back of the throat. It is different to native frog calls.

Then of course there's the matter of their poo, or more politely **scat**. The scat of a large cane toad can be 6.3 cm long! That's as big as Pete's thumb. Usually they're straight, sometimes slightly bent. They 'deposit' just one hard piece often leaving the calling card on top of rocks or mounds. Insect fragments can usually be seen and the surface is rough.

Frog scats can be large too, depending on the frog's size. They look like a mini-cigar but can't be smoked because they are too moist to light. Not to mention it would probably kill you! The scat of Fee's tree frog measured 20 mm long by 6 mm wide. It was brown and shaped like a cylinder.

Pete's sketches of cane toad scat with the green tree frog scat underneath it. He drew them to scale to show the difference in their sizes.

THE AUTOPSY AND FORENSIC REPORT

Next morning Ozzie went to the office fridge and pulled out a plastic bag. It contained two dead Pobblebonks.

'I found them right when Humph and Big Foot arrived last night. Just got them stuffed inside my coat in the nick of time.'

The kids raced off to the vet dragging him to the crime scene.

'This is really serious,' Ozzie explained. 'Two of our precious Pobblebonks have been killed. If we don't find out why, we could lose the lot.' The vet looked around carefully.

'Okay detectives, you missed the vital scene-of-crime evidence,' he said, pointing to some small green pellets. He sliced through the frogs then slit open their stomachs. Tweezers were used to remove the stomach contents. He wrote on a pad.

AUTOPSY REPORT **VICTIMS**: Pobblebonk Frogs

CRIME SCENE EVIDENCE: small green pellets
TIME OF DEATH: judging by the rigor mortis, estimated 2 pm, March 16th
TORTURE, PUNCTURE OR RESTRAINT MARKS: nil
TRACE EVIDENCE/HAIR/FIBRES: nil
STOMACH CONTENTS: snail bait
CAUSE OF DEATH: poisoning by snail bait.

At least the snails would die happy, pickled so to speak.

'The garden is the show piece of Frogsville,' Ozzie said that afternoon as the kids called into see the Mayor. 'And people are coming to see our frogs and taddies. You must get the council gardeners to stop using snail bait. We could use saucers of beer instead.'

'We could place straw and sawdust around. That would be a better idea,' Fee said. 'It would be difficult for snails to slide over.' The Mayor agreed.

'And further, can you please call a special meeting,' Ozzie demanded. 'We must educate the villagers about our frog problems.' The Mayor set a meeting for Saturday night.

POBBLEBONK DETECTIVE ACTIVITY - FROG SCIENCE

Okay aspiring Earth Detectives, entry to the *exclusive* Pobblebonk Club is on *strict* conditions. To qualify you need to carry out the Pobblebonk Detective Activities.

EARTH DETECTIVE DICTIONARY

Set up a notebook as an Earth Detective Dictionary. Rule up two columns headed Word and Meaning. You may organise it in alphabetical order or by subject e.g. frogs. Write the meanings of ten new words you have learned in the frog stories.

FROG MATTERS

- Detectives living outside Australia could choose an introduced species from their own country to research.
- Australian Detectives can use books and websites such as <frogsaustralia.net.au> and <fdrproject.com.au>. There the appearance of cane toads and how they are different to native frogs can be seen. Choose a native frog that looks similar to a cane toad. Draw labelled diagrams to show the differences.
- If you live in Toad Territory - get active! Watch out for eggs, taddies and adults. Participate in local Toad Buster events. Find out what to do if you discover a toad.
- What frog species live in your local area? Draw up a chart to show what they look like and which habitats they can be found in. Great ideas for frog surveys are at website <ecolinc.vic.edu.au/frogs>.

EARTH DETECTIVE JOURNAL

Set up an Earth Detective Journal in a notebook. Mark its cover 'Top Secret'. In it record any frog noises that you hear and when and where you heard them. Your journal can be used to record any observations about nature from now on.

Well now, how did you go? Do you rate a pass in Frog Science? Are you a qualified herp now? Do you think you qualify for membership of the club? How would you rank yourself 1-10 as an Earth Detective?

GIVING FROGS A HELPING HAND

On Saturday night the villagers crammed into the Town Hall to hear Ozzie's frog lecture.

'A fifth of the world's frogs are in big trouble,' he began, using his most dramatic voice. He projected his first drawing.

- Chemicals pollute frog habitat
- Masses of frogs are killed on roads on wet nights
- Habitat is lost due to land clearing
- Climate change affects frog habitats

FROGS ARE THE WORLD'S MOST ENDANGERED CREATURES!

- The earth's atmosphere has a layer called the **ozone layer**. It protects life on earth from harmful solar (sun) radiation. But the ozone layer has a hole in it. So then frogs absorb this harmful radiation through their thin skins.
- The biggest threat is a disease caused by a fungus that attacks protein in the frogs' skin and mouth. It occurs worldwide. Some scientists believe it will cause the worst extinction ever, due to a disease.
- Introduced creatures such as mosquito fish, carp, goldfish and cane toads compete with frogs for food and eat them too.

FROGS AND CHEMICALS

'The bad thing,' Ozzie continued, 'is that the amount of **toxin** or poison increases in an animal that eats another animal that has eaten poison. The poison builds up in every creature in the food web.'

- Snail bait is an example of a **pesticide** – a substance, often poisonous, used to kill unwanted creatures like rats.
- **Insecticides** usually in spray form, are used to kill insect pests.
- **Weedicides** are used to kill unwanted plants.
- Frogs absorb such poisons through their thin skins. That means the number of frogs in a habitat is an excellent indicator of the habitat's health. The more frogs there are then the fewer chemicals are poisoning that habitat.

'I want *everyone* to spread the word especially about chemicals and poisons,' Ozzie said, thumping his hand on the table. 'Don't you think it's sad that frogs are so endangered considering they've been around for 200 million years? Their ancestors appeared on earth 350 million years ago, even before dinosaurs! And think of all the fairy tales, kids' books and jokes based on frogs. Frogs eat serious insect pests such as mozzies that cause human diseases. In turn they provide food for snakes, birds and even the French! So if we lose them it will upset the numbers balance of other creatures. Imagine a world without them.'

SOME THINGS WE CAN ALL DO

- Know that in Australia and some other countries a licence is needed to keep frogs in captivity.
- Tadpoles and frogs should not be moved from where they are found. They may have special needs such as certain types of plants and water depths. It's better to let frogs *come* to your garden.
- Keep your cats inside at night – they love a froggy snack.
- Keep untouched areas of natural vegetation on farms, especially the lower **under storey** plants. Not everything needs to be mowed!
- Wash your car on the lawn so detergent doesn't wash into waterways.
- *Never* dispose of unwanted pet fish or plants from fish tanks in waterways. This is a huge problem that introduces more nasties into native habitats.

ALL PROBLEMS SOLVED?

'To conclude my talk, I have two treats.' Looking adoringly at Samantha, Ozzie burst into the love song from the opera, *Madam Butterfly*. Samantha sat up straight. So too did IRK. The audience was gobsmacked. This boy was something else!

'My second treat is a special dessert.' Slipping into the hall kitchen Ozzie returned with a plastic bag. And there were the Frogsville menaces. Twelve frozen toads!

'Remember when youse all thought I was out sleepwalking? I was toadnapping, laying out bowls of dog food all round the place. I put the captured toads in our office fridge to get numbed, before I froze them as Granny said. Granny insists that no matter what the creature is, it must be disposed of in the most humane way possible. And here is a new dessert recipe should any more toads appear.'

BUFO'S SPECIAL DESSERT RECIPE

Take one dozen frozen prime cut cane toads. Carefully remove poison gland. Mince finely in a blender. Mix with one cup of sugar and ......

'Oh Ozzie,' Granny gasped, jumping up to hug him. He was a hero. Everyone congratulated him, except Humph and Big Foot. Ozzie beamed. At last I am accepted he thought. Granny's ranger friend stood up.

'Hold it folks. I have found the source of the toads. Granny was *not* responsible. I believe the toads came down from Queensland in someone's trailer. Which one of you recently visited Queensland?'

Wait on, Pete thought. Doesn't Humph's daughter live there?

An old man with a hairy nose sat across the aisle. He quickly pulled his coat over his shirt. But Pete just had time to see the words, '*Queensland Perfect One Day, Brilliant The Next*'. Humph stared straight ahead, trying desperately to show no reaction. But Pete saw the reddened face, the wringing hands, the shuffling feet. And then he *knew for sure.*

Granny and the children were redeemed. Frogsville forgave the show episodes, Humph's dead chook and everything else. Samantha smiled at Ozzie. IRK allowed him to audition for the school play. (And in fact he ended up as both director and leading man!)

'Hey,' yelled Carrot Hair to Pete at lunchtime on the Monday after the meeting. 'Come and play footy with us.'

But Pete was determined to get revenge on Humph. Unfortunately the tables turned on Pete himself when a bizarre investigation was unleashed. Frogsville would gasp in horror.

POBBLEBONK DETECTIVE ACTIVITY

CHEMICAL CHECKLIST

Own up now - are poisonous chemicals being used at your place? Are old and dangerous frog-murdering chemicals hanging around? Use Ozzie's chemical checklist to do an audit at home and school. How do you score? Badly? Then you better get busy, Detectives. Where do your old unwanted chemicals go? Now don't say they go down the drain Detectives, because that makes you animal murderers. Use the checklist to see what needs to be disposed of. Get onto your local council. It will have a special place for chemical disposal.

- Household detergents and all cleaning products
- Old paints
- Bleaches, mineral turps, solvents
- Pesticides including snail bait
- Insecticides
- Rat baits/poisons
- Old pool chemicals
- Motor oils
- Garden/lawn fertilisers
- Weedicides.

DESIGN TASK

Assess the 'friendliness' of your home and school gardens to native frogs, insects and birds. Decide what improvements could be made. Do you have recycling schemes? What about native plants to encourage birds and animals? No? Then you'll be even busier.

Choose an area in which to create a native garden. (Then you will have your own mini-laboratory for earth detecting). Research the types of plants that could be used and their soil and climate needs. Design a layout and get to work! You'll be surprised at what creatures come to the garden. If Ozzie can move himself off the lounge so can you!

THE 'IA' COUNTRY BREAKFAST QUIZ

This is the 'extra hard' quiz that Fee designed to stump Samantha. Name the thirty-eight countries besides Australia, whose names end with the letters 'ia' was the *big* question.

'Ah, come on,' Carrot Hair said when he saw the question. 'Even Sherlock himself couldn't do this. We're just kids. How on earth could we do something this hard?'

'Look, it's up to you,' Fee said. 'Do you want be savvy about the world or remain an ignoramus? Use an atlas if you must.'

Samantha began working through the continents. Sweat poured down her face. She came up with only eight answers. The rest of the school combined made a list of five.

- How many can you name? Remember to score half a point for those you have to look up. Hint: eleven are in Africa, nine in Asia, twelve in Europe, two in South America and four are island countries in either the Pacific or Atlantic Oceans. Here is some help - in the following list are some of the first letters of some countries.

- **Europe**: Rom, Bulg, Aus, Croat, Lat, Lith, Est, Slova, Slove, Alb, Maced, Yugo.
- **Africa**: Tanz, Namib, Ethiop, Zamb, Alg, Tunis, Soma, Lib, Gam, Niger, Som.
- **South America**: Boli, Colom.
- **Asia** - Indo, Ind, Malay, Cambo, Mong, Saudi Ara, Russ, Geo, Arm.

- Identify the following 'ia' countries from their flag map outlines.

An 'ia' country in Europe. Remember the story, *101 Dalmatians*? These spotted dogs originally came from this country.

An 'ia' country in Africa. This country is home to Africa's highest mountain. A **dormant** or sleeping volcano, Mt. Kilimanjaro is 5 895 m high.

An 'ia' country in South America. This country is the only one in South America that has a coastline on both the Pacific Ocean and the Caribbean Sea.

An 'ia' country in Asia. This is the only country in the world that has a building on its flag. Find out what this famous building is.

- At the website <sciencekids.co.nz/sciencefacts/countries> info about these countries can be found.

SAMANTHA'S SCORE: 8/41 **FROGSVILLE SCORE: 5/41** **YOUR SCORE: /41**

CHAPTER 6: POO DUNNIT?

A NEW CASE WAS BORN

At 6 am one Saturday morning, Pete answered a thunderous knock on the door. It was Humph *again*. Armed with a rifle, he stood there his upper lip twitching.

'Where's that bleedin' dog of yours? I've come to shoot him. He's killed half me ruddy chooks overnight.'

'Calm down,' Granny said. 'It can't be Phant. He sleeps on Pete's bed, only going out through the dog door for a quick wee.'

Quoll

'Well how come he poops all over me veggie patch? What do you feed him anyway? I've never seen anything like it!'

'Look, anything could have killed those chooks – a fox, dingo, cat or quoll. Let's see what we can find out,' Granny said.

'I'll give youse one week. If you haven't solved the problem by then I'll demand the council destroy your mongrel dog. That's if I don't get to it first.'

Pete rushed off to look up the 'quoll-thing' that Granny had mentioned. He came into the kitchen trembling.

'I just listened on the Internet to the sound a quoll makes. It's terrifying. If you were camping in the bush and heard it, you'd think a lion or tiger was coming. Not that it's so loud, but the growling noise is something else. Some people even call it a tiger cat. If we have to mess around with fearsome creatures like that, Phant and I are outta here.'

'You get such wild ideas,' Granny laughed. 'It might look like a large cat, but it's not a cat or a tiger, just one of our gorgeous native animals. But it does like chicken sandwiches for lunch.'

Lean and short-legged, the quoll's fur is spotted with white blotches. It is the only native Australian animal with a spotted tail. A baby or pup is only the size of a rice grain! Pups spend eight weeks in mum's pouch then six weeks riding around on her back. A **pouch** is a sac or slit on the mother's tummy. It's a bit like a large pocket. Quolls make nests in hollow logs or trees, caves, termite mounds and old burrows.

Pete hung up the 'Do Not Disturb, Detective Conference in Progress' sign on the office door. The children sat at the main office desk.

'I've no idea where we should start,' Ozzie said. Hmm, the children sat wracking their brains.

'I know,' Fee said. 'Let's think about how Sherlock would approach the case! You know, the hound in his case, *The Hound of the Baskervilles* was a murderer too.'

'Of course, that's brilliant! He would have looked for the forensic evidence. You know things like scats, tracks, fur in and around the site. And he would have used all his senses.'

THE INVESTIGATION

DETECTIVE NOTE: 'scat' is the word that scientists use for animal 'poo'. Other polite words to use are manure and dung.

- Find out what information can be gained about animals from reading their 'signs' in the bush or the 'bush newspaper'.
- Examine the different sizes, shapes, colours and smells of the scats of the possible perps. What senses must a detective use?
- Are there clues *in* the scat that should be looked at to work out 'poo dunnit'?
- How do you tell the age of a scat is in order to determine how long ago its depositor passed by?
- Research the tracks of the possible perps. If any are similar then how are they told apart?
- Devise a way to collect evidence at the site each day.

ON THE CASE

Granny put through a call to Ranger Mike and explained the situation.

'We can't stay up all night watching for the perp to return,' she said. 'What's the best way to get evidence at the site, like tracks and scats?' Mike instructed Granny to lay a heap of sand around the chook pen. Then it would have to be raked smooth last thing each day after Humph has fed and locked up his chooks. Paw prints and scats should then be perfectly exposed.

While Granny went off to buy the sand, the kids got busy examining the tracks and scats of the possible perps.

THE GREAT 'TREASURE' HUNTS GOT UNDER WAY

'Man the tornados and fire the cannelloni, it's time to move,' Pete urged when Granny returned.

'Are your knee cartridges crook today?' he asked her, as she walked around stiffly.

'She's badly constipated,' Ozzie said. 'She has a blockage in her U bends. It's all those wretched sardines of course.' Granny you see was on her latest diet fad.

'Sardine oil is fantastic for your heart and bones,' she constantly told the kids. 'It's part of the Mediterranean diet like the Greeks and Italians eat. That's why they're so healthy.'

'Now, the best place to start our search to see what animals have been around is on the sand bars of the creek bed,' Granny said. 'Then we'll try the surrounds of Humph's chook pen.' Granny found a fox scat near her chook house and held it up to Phant's nose. Of course, he wanted to eat it didn't he?

'No, no,' Granny said. 'Smell it and go boy. Go and find some.' Phant sniffed and snorted and scratched around and wagged his tail. He passed his first test as Detective Sniffer Dog with flying colours quickly leading the way to a little 'treasure'.

'Well done boy! Look at this *magnificent* scat,' Granny said, beaming as she held it up to her nose.

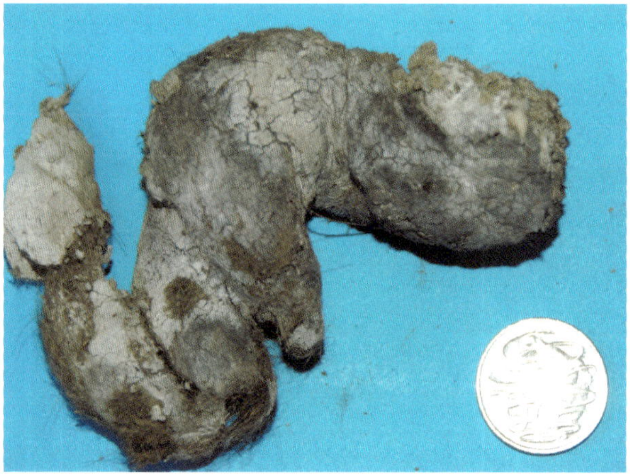

'You're not going to eat it are you?' Fee asked.

'Well you know, in Africa if you're really thirsty you can squeeze the moisture out of elephant dung and drink it!' Granny said. Fee dry-retched.

'Cute isn't it?' Ozzie said. 'Quite artistic eh? I'm sure a clothes designer could use it to create something fancy. A hat for IRK perhaps? Smells interesting eh – kind of bitter, stale and fishy. I think it may be a fox scat. Here, smell it. Take a close look,' Ozzie said, shoving the scat under Fee's nose. Phew. It was worse than the stink of his sweaty feet.

As Fee recoiled, Granny said, 'I told you – the smell is important. With a strong smell like this, we know the perp was a carnivore or meat-eater.'

'Gotta be a fox, I reckon,' Ozzie said. The fox by the way is another introduced animal like the cane toad. It was brought to Australia from Britain because the British like to hunt foxes. Foxes kill thousands of native animals every day.

'All this fuss about a bit of old scat,' Fee complained. 'Couldn't we go to town and see a movie instead? *Please*.'

'Pete pleaded – we *must* solve this problem as fast as possible. I simply can't live without Phant.'

'And I can't go round playing with poo. My cooking career could be ruined.'

'You'll all need to work flat out to solve poo dunnit,' Granny said.

Phant located a number of other scats that were carefully bagged. The kids located a number of tracks but most of them were unclear.

'Let's have morning tea,' Ozzie said, pulling out a huge lemon tart from the Udder Café. And then – Granny opened her backpack. Fee nearly fainted at the stench.

'Ah – look what I found, last week's sardine sandwich! I've been looking for that rotten thing all week.' It was rotten all right.

The kids located many scats and took photos of a variety of tracks. Phant found two scats near the chook pen but they were impossible to identify. Then it was back to the office for more hard work, under the microscope.

TRACKS AND SCATS OF THE SUSPECTS

'I can't believe this,' Pete said. 'We've spent *two* whole days on this stuff. I've only got five days left. And then there's Humph. I could murder him. Granny gave him such strict instructions about not walking on that sand trap after we've raked it smooth.' Humph had walked all over the clues left overnight. And he did the very same thing on Monday morning. Clearly he was going to destroy any forensic evidence and lay the blame on Phant at all costs.

Identifying the tracks and scats that had been found turned out to be a most difficult task. Dog and fox prints are similar. So too are cat and quoll prints. Then of course, the front and hind feet of each animal are different, aren't they? Next problem was the **straddle** or distance between the left and right footprints. And so it went on. Close observation skills were needed. Pete drew up a number of sketches of the tracks and scats of the possible suspects.

DOG AND DINGO (AUSTRALIAN WILD DOG)

Tracks: the hind foot tracks are smaller than the front ones. The central footpad of the hind foot is narrower and less clear than on the front foot. Length: 7-10 cm.

Scats: size depends on the dog's size and breed. **Feral** or wild dogs and dingos may leave scats up to 4 cm in diameter. They contain larger pieces of bone than fox scats.

RED FOX

Tracks: the straddle or distance between the left and right footprints is narrower than a dog's, often in an almost straight line. Length: 6-8 cm.

Scats: 2 cm in diameter.

Dog Front and Hind Footprint

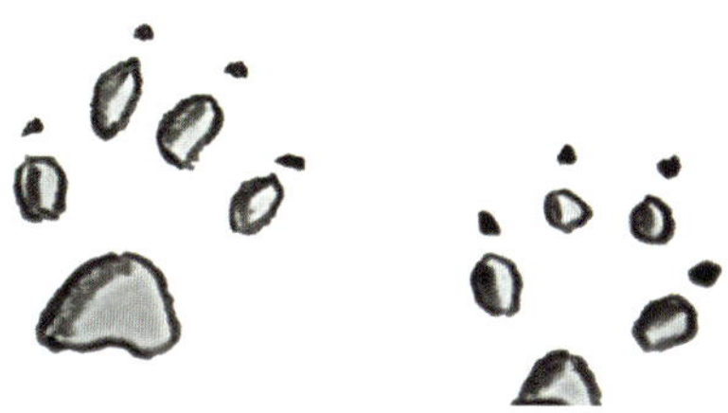

Red Fox Front and Hind Footprint

Dog Scat

Red Fox Scat

SPOT-TAILED QUOLL

Tracks: the front footprint **splays** or spreads out widely. Length: 4 cm.

Scats: dark brown and oily. The cylinder-shaped scat will be twisted at one end if fur has been eaten. A straight cylinder will result if plant matter has been eaten. Often does the 'job' in one place, especially on rocks.

CAT

Tracks: footprints are rounder than a dog or fox. The large central footpad has a semi-circle of toe pads around it. Claw marks are rare. Length: 3.5 cm.

Scats: 2-2.5 cm in diameter.

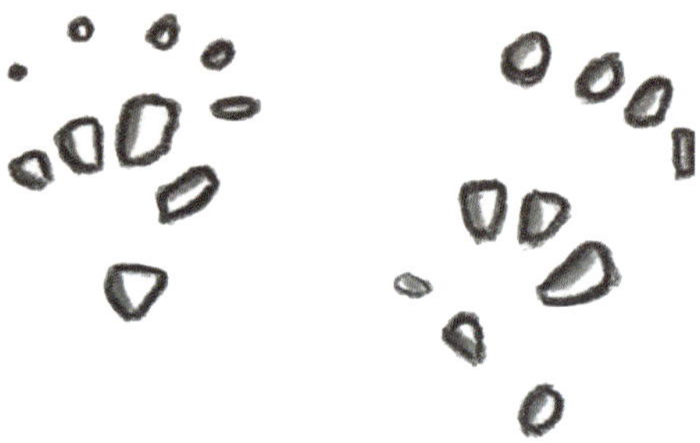

Quoll Front and Hind Footprint

Cat Front and Hind FootPrint

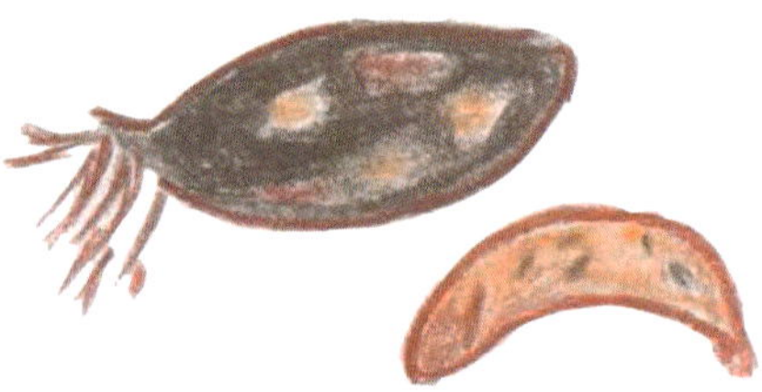

Quoll Scat

Cat Scat

POBBLEBONK DETECTIVE ACTIVITY - ANIMAL TRACKING

Now can you see what the gang was up against? This track and scat business wasn't easy. If Sherlock Holmes was trying to identify the tracks of the horrible hound in his story he would look at:

- The width of the gap between the claw marks and toe pad marks
- The number of claw marks and toe pad marks
- The number of 'sets' or rows of toe pad marks
- The shape of the claw marks and toe pads.

You too will need to look at these to do the following:

- Identify six differences between the prints of the dog and fox and six between
- the cat and quoll.
- If you had to explain how dog and cat prints are different what would you say?
- What differences can you see between the scats of the dog and red fox and the quoll and cat? And please do try to be polite.
- Choose an animal and research its tracks. What type of foot does it have? Are there claws? What does it look like underneath? Which part touches the ground? What is the size of the prints? How is the hind foot different to the front foot?

This pattern found on the beach was made by a small animal that lives in a cone-shaped shell. Finding tracks is easy.

Tracks, Scats and Other Traces by Barbara Triggs is a good reference for Australian Detectives.

Places with sand, mud or soft earth, including road or track edges and dried-up puddles are good for finding tracks. Don't use the excuse there's no bush land where you live. Check out the nearest park, beach, river or creek bank, zoo or even schoolyard. Begin with something simple, like cat and dog tracks.

Can't find anything? Bird tracks are easy to find. Try looking for trails left by ants, slugs, snails and lizards. Record all findings in your journal and include sketches or photos. What do reckon Sherlock would think of your efforts?

OTHER SIGNS IN THE BUSH NEWSPAPER

Animals leave many other signs of their presence. Koalas leave scratch marks as they climb tree trunks. Sugar gliders make slash marks on tree trunks where they scratch for tree sap. Bandicoots leave holes where they dig for roots. Kangaroos flatten the grass where they lie down. Get active Detectives and see what you can find.

GRANNY'S FAMOUS TALK

Fee was asleep over her sums *again* on Monday morning.

'Well what have you been up to *this* weekend?' IRK spat. 'What are you and Granny working on at the moment?'

'It's all about poo.'

'Poo?' IRK said, turning white. 'Oh, you mean her cures for constipation and piles,' she cackled.

'No I mean she's an expert at using animal signs like their dung, to track them. She's lived in Africa you know.'

Fee related the story of Humph's chooks and the weekend's events. The class was rapt. What a strange subject this all was!

'Please,' Carrot Hair said. 'Can Granny give us a talk on animals and their poo?'

'Definitely not, it is not a fit subject for my students,' IRK said, feeling sick. But the class pestered all day and she caved in, anything for peace.

Next day Granny bustled into the school, complete with scat samples. Samantha immediately demanded that Granny draw up a Special Breakfast Quiz. It must be done in strict secrecy. Fee must not know its contents.

'Fine,' Granny said. 'And while we're at it, why don't we enter the school in the NSW Geography Competition?' Yes, yes the students begged.

THE IMPORTANCE OF ANIMAL DUNG!

'Now let's begin with the absolute basics. Animal dung plays a vital part in the relationships between plants, animals and their environment. Animal dung contains **nutrients** or goodies such as nitrogen and calcium. Every living thing needs these nutrients. Plants like my precious Brussels sprouts must be fertilised by animal dung to grow. Then animals eat the plants and the nutrients are passed onto them. And so on. It's called the **nutrient cycle**.'

'What!' Samantha shrieked. 'Are you telling us that everything we eat has dung in it?'

'No,' Granny laughed. 'It works like this.'

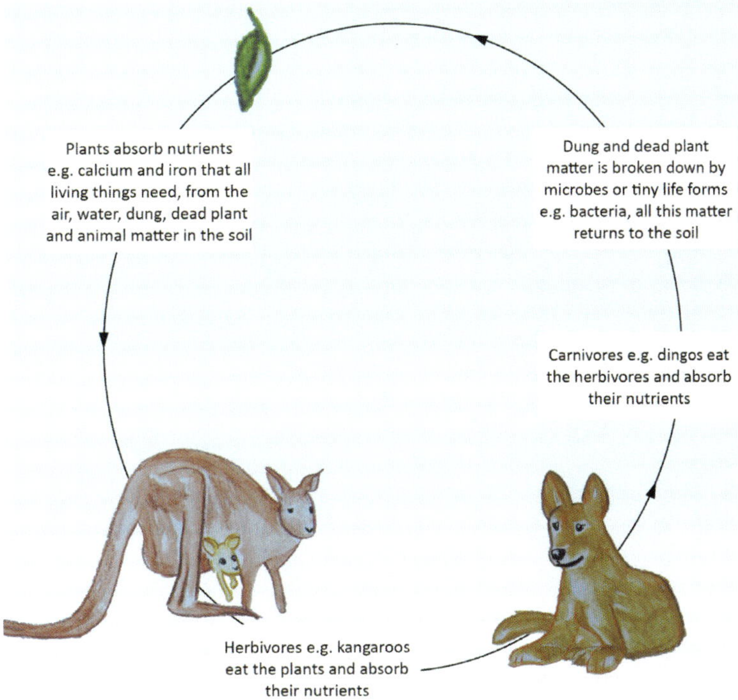

Nutrient Cycle

'I told you so,' Pete said joyfully. 'Clarence my cockroach *is* important. He's part of this whole cycle. Did you know he's also called a Giant Litter Bug? That's because he feeds on dried leaf litter. By doing this he breaks down the goodies in the leaves. When he poos, all those goodies are returned to the soil. This helps plants to grow – even our pumpkins!'

Rhinoceros Cockroach

Almost as big as the palm of Pete's hand at 80 mm long, a rhinoceros cockroach is the world's heaviest **species** or type of cockroach. It weighs up to 35 grams. Get a look at the spines on its feet. These flick the soil out behind the roach as it burrows. Can you see the 'shield' that sits over its head? This acts like a shovel for burrowing! No wonder it needs that because the burrow can be 6 m long!

'He's right,' Granny said, looking at the disbelief on Samantha's face. '*Every* creature plays a role of some kind in nature. And by the way, microbes make up about one-third of animal waste including yours and mine.'

'Whaaat? You mean there's living things in poo?' Things were getting worse by the minute. But then Granny told the kids all this important stuff.

Undigested seeds in dung make tasty leftovers for birds and animals!

It turned out animal dung is:

• *Food!* Creatures such as fish and dung beetles eat it. Grizzly bears spend winter **hibernating** in dens. This means that they go into a deep sleep and don't eat. After so long without food, they must get good-guy bacteria into their gut. Then they can begin normal eating again. So what's the first thing they eat: moose and deer dung that contain the bacteria!

• Vital for spreading seeds so that new plants can grow. Some tough-skinned seeds must even pass through an animal's gut before they can **germinate** or sprout. The seed comes out the other end fertilised, watered and with a thinner skin!

• Widely used to fertilise gardens and crops, like the cow dung used at The Pumpkin Patch to grow the veggies. Do you know by the way that a cow may drop up to fifteen cow pats a day weighing 29.5 kg? That's about 908 kg a year to fertilise the ground!

ANIMAL SCATS

'Okay, how about you ask me some questions about animal scats now?' Granny said.

'How can you tell different animals from their scats? Aren't they all the same?' Carrot Hair asked, trying to be funny.

'Oh no! Scats come in all shapes, colours and sizes. Every animal species has a different shaped scat according to its diet, bowel or intestine size and the diameter of its sphincter muscle. **A sphincter muscle** is a ring of muscle around the opening of a hollow organ such as an intestine.'

'Sometimes you can only tell what animal has done the deed from the smell. That is a special skill. **Consistency** is important too.'

'What do you mean?' Carrot Hair asked.

'You know, whether it is sloppy or firm. Like the consistency of those famous lemon puddings Miss Ramsbotham makes. They're light and fluffy.'

Thanks very much, IRK thought. I'll never be able to look another pudding in the eye.

'But look,' Granny said. 'Most of you come from dairy farms. You should know about the consistency of your cowpats. It is most important in making sure they are healthy. Now are any of you having soup, pies, custard or biscuits at dinner tonight? I want you to think about this consistency business.'

Not realising what Granny was on about Samantha flung her arm in the air. Fee snickered. Wait till you see what this is about!

'Mum's cooking her legendary beef and veggie pie tonight!'

'That's wonderful. You pay extra attention now. Here we go.'

CONSISTENCY OF ANIMAL SCATS

Watery: very liquid, consistency between water and a light soup. Dung may shoot out in an arc from the cow. Your cow may be eating too much protein.

Custardy: runny, doesn't form a pile, is less than 2.5 cm high, splatters when it hits the ground. Your cow is eating too much young grass.

Like a pie: piles up to 5 cm, in the rough shape of a pie with a small pit in the middle. The dung makes a plopping sound as it reaches the ground. This is the ideal situation for your cow.

Hard: dung is thick and piles up over 5 cm. Your cow may be eating too much older grass.

Fancy biscuits: firm biscuit-like stack. Your cow may have a blockage in its digestive tract and needs more nutritious food.

'It is important to be able to tell the age of a scat too. In order to meet Humph's deadline, the kids have had to learn this very fast. Otherwise they're wasting time on months-old scats.'

Fresh scats: moist outside and in. A thin liquid film shows that a scat was deposited in the last 12 hours. Fresh herbivore scats are dark black, brown or green.

A few days old: dry on the outside with some moisture inside.

Weeks or months old: are broken up, no moisture, bleached of colour. In hot weather bleaching occurs within two days. In colder weather it takes several weeks.

First parts to decay: meat and skin decay first. Bones, coarse hairs and grasses take months.

'Now look at this magnificent carnivore specimen,' Granny said, laying out the scats on IRK's desk.

CARNIVORE SCAT

Carnivore scat is often whitish from the calcium in the bones of the **prey** or the animal it has eaten. If flesh and blood has been eaten, the scat will be black or dark reddish. Some scats are cylinder-shaped, often pointed at one end. Some may be sausage-shaped.

'Carnivore scat has a nasty, strong smell. It is worst if the animal has eaten **carrion** or rotting flesh like you would find in a road kill several days old. To work out poo dunnit, the inside of the scat must be looked at too. You will need tweezers and possibly a microscope for this. Feathers, fur, eggshells, reptile scales, teeth, insect parts, hair and bones may be in there,' Granny said. Samantha's stomach did a double flip for the second time.

HERBIVORE SCAT

This scat also smells, but it is more of an earthy smell. Herbivore scat is brownish or greenish coloured but fades over time. If the plant matter eaten was wet, the scat will be a shapeless splotch. The emu that deposited this scat in the photo had eaten moist red berries. Bits of plant matter, fruit skins and seed can be present. Drier plant matter results in scat that looks like **pellets** or small round balls. Rabbit scat is a good example.

'Do animals poo in different ways?' came another question. 'I mean they don't sit on toilets like us,' a boy snickered.

'Well, some animals *do* have toilets. They 'go' in one place. That tells other animals this is *my* territory. There are many strange habits. The wombat for example, likes to do its business on a rock or mound. That probably advertises his presence a little more.'

'Let me tell you some more interesting things. Some animals for example dogs, clench their buttocks during the act, so the scat becomes pinched off like a string of sausages. Antarctica's Gentoo Penguins are into **projectile pooing**. They fire it up to 38 cm away to keep their bodies clean! Too bad if some other poor penguin is in the way eh! Bird poo by the way is known as **guano**.'

Samantha checked her dictionary. 'Projectile' – a self-propelled missile it said. She wished she had one to fire at Granny.

'And finally, some animals even eat their own dung!'

KOALAS AND RABBITS EAT THEIR OWN DUNG!

When a rabbit eats, food particles are sorted into sizes in its large intestine. The larger coarser particles that can't be **digested** or broken down, force the smaller digestible ones back up the intestine. They collect in a sac while the larger ones are **excreted,** or passed out of the body. In the sac the good stuff **ferments** or 'cooks up' with the help of yeast, bacteria and other goodies. The result is soft, shiny clumps of sweet smelling 'night poo'.

The rabbit eats this straight from its anus to put all the goodies back into its gut! The female koala produces this same night poo when weaning her joey that eats this dung. Truly! Heaps of vitamins, minerals, proteins and the right microbes prepare the joey's gut for its new diet of eucalypt leaves. About pea-size, the dung is softer than the koala's normal dung.

POBBLEBONK DETECTIVE ACTIVITY - POO DONE THIS ONE?

Does this scat belong to a herbivore or carnivore? What has it eaten? How old would you estimate the scat to be? How would you describe its shape, colour and consistency? Use the twenty-cent piece to work out the length and width of the three large pieces.

THE AFTERMATH

IRK felt horrified by Granny's talk as she cleaned up all the bits of scat from her desk. But she had to admit the woman knew her stuff. There was no way she could have tripped her up. The kids loved it. Well, not quite all of them because three, including Samantha ended up in sickbay for the rest of the day. Samantha pleaded with her Mum to make toast and vegemite for dinner that night. At least that had nothing to do with scats, although she bet Granny could come up with *some* comparison.

The students could talk of nothing else for weeks. Granny was now booked up to give field lessons at The Pumpkin Patch. Her talk went down in the annals of Frogsville Central School history.

The first thing new students were asked was 'have you heard about Granny's famous talk?'

As for the Special Breakfast Quiz, it is at the end of the chapter. Samantha beat Fee by one point. Can you better their scores? Fee was angry of course. How much *more* work would she have to do to beat her rival?

COULD PHANT BE POSTED TO SYDNEY?

Granny was awoken at dawn by rifle shots, crack, crack, crack. Peeking out the window she saw Humph firing shots at tin cans lined up on his fence. Oh dear. Perhaps a cup of tea might help me she thought.

As she walked into the kitchen, Pete was trying to lift Phant into a large cardboard box. The floor was strewn with boxes of different sizes, ropes, tapes and bubble wrap. Phant's bowl and cans of dog food were stacked beside the box.

'What on earth is going on?'

'I'm posting Phant down to Mum in Sydney. But I'm worried how he's gonna breathe or drink or eat or wee in a box. I dunno what to do!' Pete threw his arms around the dog's neck and broke down in wracking sobs. Phant whined pitifully and licked his tears away.

'You can't post him darling. You can't put living creatures in the post.'

'Well do you know someone who would hide him for a few days?'

Ozzie and Fee had come out to see what the racket was.

'You're forgetting that the village hates Phant's guts,' Ozzie said. 'They ain't never gonna forget that he ruined their possible moment of glory in the footie match. They'd hand him over to Humph with pleasure.'

'Right, that's it,' Granny said. 'Stay home from school today and we'll work flat out.'

Could Phant be saved?

THE SPECIAL BREAKFAST QUIZ: AUSTRALIA'S NEIGHBOURS

The morning after Granny's famous talk she delivered a sealed envelope to the school. IRK opened the envelope as all the bright-eyed students craned forward. Here it was:

- Identify the four countries from their flag map outlines below. They are Australia's closest neighbours.
- Match these capitals to the countries: Dili, Wellington, Jakarta, Port Moresby.
- Which country has two main islands named North Island and South Island?
- In which country would you find the island of Bali?
- One of the maps contains these islands: Sumatra, Java, Sulawesi – locate each of these islands on the map.
- Name the biggest island in the above country.
- Which two of the countries have several volcanoes?
- Which country is separated from Australia by the Arafura Sea?
- The Tasman Sea separates Australia from which neighbour?
- Which of the four countries has the biggest population?
- In which country would you find the city of Christchurch that was struck by two major earthquakes in 2011?

AUSTRALIA'S CLOSE NEIGHBOURS

FEE'S SCORE: 10/23 **SAMANTHA'S SCORE**: 11/23 **YOUR SCORE**: /23

CHAPTER 7: WOULD THE PHANTOM BE SAVED?

HUMPH GOT CRANKIER

'While we've got a little spare time, let's set up an experiment on the age of animal scats,' Ozzie said. 'Then if we need to use Poo Dunnit skills again, we'll be experts.'

'Hmm,' Pete pondered. 'I imagine we need to lay the scats out in different places and weather conditions over a period of time. Then we'll need to observe how long it takes them to dry out. Let's lay out the samples we've already collected, on the front lawn.'

And yes – right then up drove Humph, 'how much progress have you made?' he roared. 'Ya got two more nights or your dog is a goner.'

'What are ya up to anyway?' he said, eyes bulging with curiosity.

'We're collecting animal poos,' Ozzie wound him up.

'Poos? Whatever for?'

'To see what's in them and work out how old they are.'

'What's in em? I can damn well tell you what's in em. What's your lunatic granny think about this?'

'*She's* writing a book about it. And after all Humph, we *are* trying to identify your chook murderer.'

'I told you this family is a biscuit short of a morning tea,' Humph grunted to his wife Mavis. Phant snarled then lifted a leg, spraying out a stream of hot yellow liquid.

'Couldn't you just go to the beach or play Monopoly or do something that *regular* kids do? And look what your dog's done on me good R. M. Williams boots,' he growled.

'I'll get yer yet you mongrel.' If only I could give you a dam good kick up the whatsa he thought.

'By the way Humph, dya know that in Asia bat poo is used to cure baldness? You could get some and we could find out how to put it on for you,' Pete stirred on. 'Anyway, what's an old coot? That's what Granny said you are.'

'This is the last straw. Rotten woman, I'll get her yet.' He screamed off, taking two centimetres of rubber off the tyres of his battered FJ Holden. Phant smiled his big wide grin in triumph, showing pink and black all the way down to his tonsils. But it wasn't a laughing matter.

Mavis

That afternoon Humph fired more shots. Crack, crack, crack, they rang through the air echoing in the hills. Pete was at nine out of ten on the panic scale. And next thing, he discovered pieces of meat along the fence line. He was sure they were poisoned. Just then there was an apparition on the other side of the fence, like a vision of the Creature from the Deep. Wearing a dressing gown, pyjamas and hair curlers, it had no teeth, a sunken mouth and no lips without the teeth. It was armed with a shotgun. Phant took one look, bolted under the fence and lunged at its neck.

'Phant, Phant it's Mavis, it's Mavis!' Pete screamed. Recognition sparked just in the nick of time. Phant backed off looking sheepish and embarrassed. Mavis was armed with a shotgun.

THE EVENTS OF DAY SIX

Now it was Day Six. Humph belted the door down at daylight.

'I've lost another chook overnight. Do you know how much those Rhode Island Red Hens are worth? I'm goin' straight to see my lawyer.'

Pete took the others aside.

'I've got something to tell you,' he gasped between sobs. 'Last night I took Phant out for a pee. But he bolted before I got the lead round his neck and was gone for half an hour. He came back with part of a dead chook in his jaws. I buried it in the pumpkin patch.'

'Right,' Granny said wiping her brow. 'I'm still sure Phant is not our murderer. We've got one alternative left and that's to spend the *whole* night hidden at the chook pen. I need you to avoid showering, using soap or anything else smelly that might give our presence away to an animal. Spend the day outside and get as earthy-smelling as you can.'

'Wow!' Ozzie said. 'Does that mean I can go without a shower for the whole week?' Granny's look gave him the answer.

Just before dark they gathered up torches, jackets and snacks. They were all set to go. But where were Pete and Phant? Ozzie discovered Pete's school backpack was gone. So too was Granny's large travel rucksack. Pete's stash of pocket money was missing along with all the cans of Chum from the pantry. Granny called the police. The farm and surrounds were searched but no boy and dog were found.

Three weary bodies then sat out the rest of the night behind the bushes, nudging each other to keep awake. At 1 am Granny prodded the others and pointed.

And there was old foxy loxy making his way to the pen. They watched as it began digging a hole at the fence. The chooks flapped around, cackling and screaming blue murder. Ozzie yelled and hunted the fox away, flapping his arms. Granny phoned the ranger next morning to bring up a trap. Returning home there was no news of Pete. A message was being broadcast on the TV and radio.

MISSING IN ACTION

Police hold grave concerns for the safety of an eight-year old boy, Pete Mathieson. Pete is an Earth Detective. It is feared that he may have gone missing in relation to an investigation he is working on. Pete disappeared from Frogsville on the Mid North Coast last night together with his dog, a black and ginger Staffordshire terrier. The dog answers to the name of Phantom. It is believed Pete is wearing khaki shorts and shirt and is carrying a blue school backpack and a large black travel rucksack. Anyone sighting the boy is asked to phone the police urgently. The boy's granny pleads with him if he hears this message to come home. The chook murderer has been found. It is *not* your dog.

PBL NEWS APRIL 2nd

TROUBLE AT BROADMEADOW

Later that day Granny answered the phone for the 200th time. Would it be another false sighting of Pete?

'It's the Broadmeadow stationmaster here. Do you have a grandson named Pete?'

'Oh,' Granny said, her shaking hands dropping the phone. Then, '*please* tell me you have found him. Half NSW is looking for him.'

'Oh yes we have found him. He's about to be arrested.'

'What on earth for? He's just a little boy.'

'Firstly he's been riding on the train without a ticket. And secondly he had a dog stuffed in a big rucksack. Taking animals on trains is illegal.'

'Oh please,' Granny pleaded, relating the whole sorry story. Thankfully the mess got sorted. The family dashed to Broadmeadow.

'Everything was okay,' Pete sobbed, 'until this silly old woman saw Phant stick his head out of the rucksack and reported it. We were thrown off the train and had to sit on the platform alone all night. Where are Phant and I gonna go now?'

'It's fine to come home now. The chook murderer has been caught and despatched.'

THE UNUSUAL DISCOVERIES

After the fuss about Poo Dunnit settled down, Granny took the kids spotlighting for several nights. Unusual scats that they had found lead them to believe there were other animals around. Once again they crept out in the dark, trying to walk in dead silence. That was hard for Ozzie of course. But it was so exciting, creeping around in such silence that you could hear your own heart beating! Then – stop – what was that? Some leaves rustled. Could they find the source? Where on earth would you look amongst that mass of green leaves?

Granny was an expert of course. It didn't take her long to locate animals, picking up their red eye shine. She had a special torch so that the animals' eyes wouldn't be hurt. And so that the animals wouldn't get stressed the kids weren't allowed to look for too long. The animals were ones the kids had never heard of. Neither had anyone else in Frogsville. And not many Australians are familiar with these lesser-known animals either.

It wasn't just the school kids begging for talks from the Detectives, the whole village was. And so a series of talks began on Saturday nights. Every single villager, even Humph attended. Ozzie insisted that everyone present must do all the Detective Activities. These are some of the animals that were found.

THE HERBIVORES

Rufous Bettong

Rufous Bettong – a Tiny Kangaroo

This animal is a **Rat-kangaroo**. It belongs to a group of very small kangaroos. The Bettong weighs only 3.35 kg and is 38 cm long. No one had any idea kangaroos could be so small. Most Rat-kangaroos are even smaller than this. It is an **omnivore**, eating both plant *and* animal matter. The word **rufous** means reddish brown referring to the fur colour.

The bettong builds a cone-shaped nest with a front door 10 cm across. The building materials are grass and crushed up bark. The site is under logs, shrubs or in dense grass. So how does the animal carry this material to the building site? Curled up in its tail of course!

Sugar Glider – a Possum That Can Glide Fifty Metres or More!

Gliders are members of the possum family. They glide through the treetops to feed on nectar. A **membrane** or thin tissue stretches from the fifth finger to the first toe. To glide the animal just spreads its arms and legs and floats downwards using the membrane as 'wings' and its tail to steer!

Gliders are a friendly lot. They build **communal** or shared nests of up to seven adults and their young in tree hollows. Imagine the chaos of that, especially at feeding time! Nests are bowl-shaped and made of eucalypt leaves.

Sugar Glider

Eastern Pygmy-possum – Small Enough to Fit in Your Hand!

Ranger Mike brought a pygmy possum to the meeting. He rescued it when it fell out of a tree and was injured. Soon it would be fit enough to return to the forest. Everyone had to sit still and be quiet so that the animal would not be stressed. A few people were allowed to hold it in their hand. The first was Humph.

'Oh, it's so beautiful,' he said. Pete saw tears well in his eyes. Was Humph sick?

The tiny mouse-sized possum weighed only about as much as a couple of large spoons of sugar. **Pygmy** means under-sized. Measuring just 8 cm long, it eats insects and nectar.

Its nest, only 6 cm in diameter, is made of torn-up bark or grass in small tree or stump hollows.

Eastern Pygmy Possum
Reproduced by Permission of Oxford University Press Australia and New Zealand from a Field Guide to Mammals of Australia by Peter Menkhorst and Frank Knight ©2001 Frank Knight

THE CARNIVORES

Brush-tailed Phascogale – a Type of Wambenger!

Hey now, the wambenger is not a fancy type of hamburger! It is a rat-sized animal measuring 20 cm long. So *please* be careful when you're putting out rat baits and traps. This is a boy and he weighs a tiny 310 grams! Living in trees, he uses his fingers to find goodies under bark and in cracks.

Wambengers line a hole in a tree or stump with bark or leaves. This family is in trouble because towns, farms and roads have broken up their habitat.

Brush-tailed Phascogale
Reproduced by Permission of Oxford University Press Australia and New Zealand from a Field Guide to Mammals of Australia by Peter Menkhorst and Frank Knight ©2001 Frank Knight

Spot-tailed Quoll

This animal was described in Chapter 6 when it was a suspect in Poo Dunnit. Its preferred real estate is a comfy den in caves, termite mounds, old burrows or hollow logs or tree hollows. Landlords like Humph cut down their old or dead trees where all the hollows are, evicting the tenants. Then no hollows are left for quoll houses. Unless the quoll can rent another house nearby it will die because it can't move into another quoll's territory to live or feed. This is the same situation for koalas and several other tree-dwelling animals.

POBBLEBONK DETECTIVE ACTIVITY - DESCRIBING ANIMALS

Observe the animal pictures above. Describe the appearance of the phascogale. Hint: describe its colour, feet, number of toes, whiskers, size and colour of the ears, shape of the head, length and nature of the tail.

- Describe the differences between the glider and pygmy possum.
- Describe four things about the appearance of the bettong.
- Which animals (or birds) might use tree hollows around where you live?
- What other animals and birds may make their homes in hollow logs, abandoned bird nests or termite mounds?

ALARMING NEWS WAS DISCOVERED

As the gang was researching their animals, some alarming information was unearthed.

When the numbers of a species becomes low, it faces the risk of becoming extinct. There are several words to describe how bad this risk is:

- **Extinct**: died out, none left.
- **Critically endangered**: a very high risk of extinction.
- **Endangered**: in danger of becoming extinct.
- **Vulnerable:** not yet endangered, but numbers continue to fall.

Australian mammals including extinct ones can be explored at <australianmuseum.net.au/mammals>.

Since European people settled in Australia in 1788, about fifty animal and bird species have become extinct. This includes eleven members of the kangaroo family. Australia has more endangered species than any other continent. Sixty plants are extinct. A whopping ninety-six animal species are critically endangered. Over 1 000 plants are also at risk.

SOME CAUSES OF THIS PROBLEM

- When land is cleared for settlement, farms or mines, and forests are logged, habitat is lost. This has been the biggest cause of extinctions in the past. For example, only 10 % of Australia's original rainforest cover remains.
- But now there is an equally as bad problem. Introduced predators such as cane toads, cats, dogs, and foxes kill millions of native animals each year. Animals such as goats, camels and rabbits compete with native species for habitat, food and shelter.
- An animal may need a special food or habitat. If these disappear, the animal will not survive. An example is the spectacled flying fox that lives only in rainforests. The more rainforest that is cleared, the fewer flying foxes there will be.

PUMPKIN PATCH POST - MARSUPIALS

Australia has more mammal families than any other continent. **Mammals** are animals that give birth to live young e.g. humans, horses and elephants. The young feed on the mother's milk. But most Australian mammals are also **marsupials** e.g. kangaroos and koalas.

Seven out of the world's nine marsupial families are found only in Australia and New Guinea. The other two families are possums and opossums. They live in North and South America.

All the animals that the kids found on the farm are marsupials. Now what does that strange name mean? It comes from the word 'marsupium' or pouch. A **pouch** is like a small sac on the mother's belly or sometimes a flap of skin. Some mothers don't have a pouch, but carry the joeys attached to their teats.

Marsupial mums give no sign that it's time to ring the ambulance and go to the labour ward. Their bellies don't swell like other mammals. For example, when her 'baby' is due, the kangaroo mum begins licking her pouch cleaning out the nursery, for a few minutes here and there. After some time she goes into manic cleaning mode. That nursery must be spotless.

Now about joey's toilet routine: mum has to stimulate it to make it go to the toilet. Then she licks up all the mess and swallows it. Otherwise that nursery is gonna be a ... well you-know-what.

Unlike other mammals, a **joey** or marsupial baby is born in a highly undeveloped state. It isn't in mum's uterus for long before it is born. This means there is no need for Mum to support the growth of a **foetus** or undeveloped baby for a long time if there is drought and lack of food. The pay off for joey is that it can stay in mum's pouch for a long time and drink her milk. Sadly though, mum's milk has no chocolate flavouring.

When joey is ready to be born, the kangaroo mum sits on her bottom with her tail between her legs. She licks and cleans a passage to her pouch. The wet hair allows joey to grasp its way. For joey it is like a climb to Mt. Everest. If it falls off, it's a goner. Joey finds its way to the pouch by following the scent of the milk bar. The size of a jellybean or less, it is born blind and without fur. The pouch will be joey's home until it can look after itself. Here it is protected from predators.

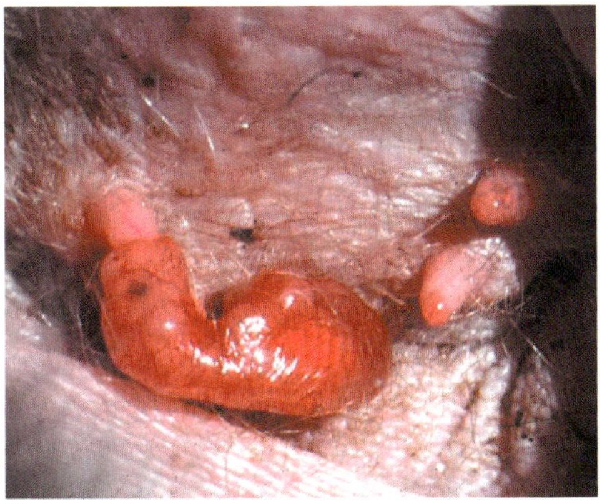

In the pouch joey latches onto a teat that swells firmly in its mouth. This keeps it securely in place while its mother moves around.
Photograph by Professor Geoff Shaw, University of Melbourne.

Other female mammals have only one uterus in which a baby grows. But marsupials have two! This is a survival strategy. Joeys do not survive in severe drought. Even in a mild drought over 80% may die.

So as soon as a joey leaves the uterus for mum's pouch, another baby is waiting to develop, just in case. Amazingly, females can have three young at the same time. One can be in the pouch, one out of the pouch and one a fertilised egg held in the uterus waiting to develop.

THE BIG FOOT FAMILY

Ozzie gave this report to one of the meetings. He's getting good enough to be a television presenter Granny thought.

Pete's sketch of a red kangaroo hind footprint

'Kangaroos and wallabies belong to a family known as **macropods**,' he explained. 'Macro means large and pod means feet, in other words – large feet. This refers to the long hind feet and toes. Even though the family members vary in size, they all have big feet, even the little Rat-kangaroo.'

This family includes some weird names like **wallaroos, potoroos and quokkas**. Wallaroos are large stocky kangaroos that live in hilly country. Potoroos are rabbit-sized. All three species of them are threatened. The quokka is a small member of the family that lives only on a few islands off the Western Australian coast. The strange name 'kangaroo' comes from the name given to the animal by the Guugu Yimithurr people of northern Queensland.

At the 'small end' of the family are animals such as the Mala that weighs only 1.3 kg. At the 'big end' are the giant male red kangaroos that weigh over 90 kg and stand 1.8 m tall. Kangaroos can hop at speeds of 56 km an hour and up to 70 km over short distances. They are superb athletes, easily able to win the high jump and long jump at the Olympic Games!

Kangaroos must be able to escape predators and also to move large distances to find food and water. With joey secure in the pouch, mum doesn't have to wait for it to keep up with her.

Kangaroos and wallabies are the only large animals to use hopping as a way of moving.

When mum is hopping, latching onto that teat in mum's pouch is important. It can be a rough ride in that pouch.

'Hey Mum! Slow down. I need a milkshake and you could do with a coffee break. You're breaking the speed limit. You haven't given me enough time to get in the baby seat. I got in in such a hurry. My left foot is stuck over my head and my tail's hanging out.'

Wallaby

So what's the difference between kangaroos and wallabies?

In general, wallabies are smaller. They have a shorter distance between their ankles and knees. A kangaroo's legs are built for speed in open country. A wallaby's more compact legs are built for movement in forested areas.

A wallaby's coat is usually brighter with two to three different colours. For a more scientific way to tell the two animals apart though, you'll have to get them to open their mouths and say 'aaah'. They have different teeth. Wallaby teeth are flat for grinding leaves. Kangaroo teeth are slightly sharper for snipping off grass.

'Okay, nobody has asked about kangaroo scat yet.' It was Pete's turn to do some reporting. Oh yeah, like everyone was *dying* to know about this tantalising topic.

The calling cards of kangaroos and wallabies are neat little cubes, usually about eight of them.

KANGAROOS THAT LIVE IN TREES

'Now, we bet you don't know that there are kangaroos that live in trees,' Fee added.

'You're having hallucinations girlie,' Humph said. 'You've been smelling too much animal dung! Whoever heard of kangaroos living in trees? Next you'll tell us koalas can fly!'

But it is true! Two types of tree kangaroo live in the rainforests of northern Queensland. These fellas can jump from tree to tree. The large tail helps them to balance.

MONOTREMES: A JOKE?

'I've got a platypus in my creek,' a lonely old farmer said one Saturday night. 'Can you give us a report on that next week?' After all there was *nothing* to do in Frogsville on Saturday nights. Besides which he loved the mini concert that Ozzie gave at the end of each night. I'm getting a free music education too he thought. And he just couldn't wait to get stuck into Fee's pumpkin scones at supper.

Of course the more limelight Ozzie got, the better, so he prepared yet another report.

The duck-billed platypus belongs to a most strange mob, he reported. It is one of only three mammals in the world classed as **monotremes.** The young feed on the mother's milk like all mammals. The difference is that they are laid as eggs.

When early settlers sent drawings of the platypus back to England, people thought it was a joke. That strange bill was pasted on, they insisted! The bill is broad, flat and hairless, similar to a duck's. Add webbed feet and a broad, flat tail that helps in swimming and you've got a bizarre-looking animal. The platypus uses its bill to scoop up food like worms and small shellfish.

Platypuses are small, growing only from 41-56 cm long, including the 10-13 cm long tail. Weighing only about 2.3 kg, they appear heavier because of their thick coat of brown fur. They live in stream-bank burrows as long as 26 m.

During the mating season, the female builds a nest of leaves and grass at the end of her burrow. Before laying between one and three eggs, she puts up the 'Keep Out' sign. The eggs measure about 1.3 cm in diameter and have a leathery shell. Eggs hatch after about ten days. The young remain in the burrow for four months.

Platypus

The other two monotremes are both echidna species – one found in Australia, one in New Guinea. Echidnas (ee-kid-nas) are a bit like porcupines or hedgehogs. They look like a ball of spikes that waddles like a duck. Echidnas are also called spiny anteaters. A long tongue and sticky saliva mean they can easily lick up ants. The long, thin snout helps them to poke into ants' nests. Their tracks are easy to tell. They have an unusual hind foot with long claws that curve backwards.

Echidna

Pete's sketch – Echidna footprint

DO NOT FEED THE WILDLIFE!

'By the way, you should never feed kangaroos or any other wildlife for that matter,' Fee stressed. 'You may think you are doing them a favour, but food not natural to their diet can kill them. Lots of people like to feed bread to kangaroos for example. But bread has yeast that produces a chemical reaction in the roo's gut. This causes many problems including gum infections. Some roos may die because their teeth are affected and they can no longer chew.'

SNAPSHOTS OF AUSTRALIA'S PAST – A FOUR BILLION YEAR JOURNEY

Ozzie had never worked so hard in his life and needed a break. It wasn't just the research but now the villagers wanted him to form a choir too.

'You give the next talk Granny and I'll just do the singing.'

So Granny prepared a talk about the past.

'Australia's animals were different in the past. Fifteen million years ago, most of Australia was a tropical paradise covered with rainforest. Six types of koalas lived in this paradise that is now covered by deserts. Twelve croc species lived there too. One was like an alligator with a broad, flat snout. Another was a dwarf species. Along with freshwater dolphins, they lived in a chain of inland lakes. Scientists know this because of fossils.'

'During the **Ice Ages** when the earth's temperatures dropped, much of Australia was buried under billions of tonnes of ice. It's hard to imagine isn't it that the environment changes so much over time?'

The Pilbara is one of the world's two oldest pieces of crust.

'What codswallop,' Humph whispered to Mavis.

'For starters, the earth's climate has changed many times. And earth's crust is like a heap of broken jigsaw pieces. They have moved around over time, changing the shape of every continent. Sea levels have risen and fallen too. At the end of the last Ice Age 10 000 years ago, sea level rose much higher. The coastlines of all countries were changed.'

Granny showed a series of pictures.

FRAME 1 – 4.3 BILLION YEARS AGO

The earth's crust is broken into jigsaw-like pieces that move around over time. The crust that makes up the Pilbara in Western Australia and the Yilgarn to its south was all there was to Australia. These are the earth's oldest pieces of crust (besides you Humph, you old coot she thought). In the Pilbara, 3.8 billion year old fossils have been found. The Yilgarn has rock crystals dated at 4.1 billion years old.

Now these old guys liked to travel. The liquid currents under the earth's crust have carried them all the way between the north and south poles twice! Over time, lots of other pieces of crust were added and subtracted.

FRAME 2 – 290 MILLION YEARS AGO

Pangaea

All the world's landmasses were joined in a 'super-continent' known as **Pangaea**. The northern part was known as **Laurasia**. Australia was located in the southern part, known as **Gondwana**.

Laurasia and Gondwana

FRAME 3 – 153 MILLION YEARS AGO

Huge movements in the earth's crust broke up Pangaea. Laurasia and Gondwana got a divorce. South America, Africa and Australia were some of the landmasses making up Gondwana. Australia and Antarctica broke away. They had the world's longest love affair, staying together for almost 100 million years.

FRAME 4 – 100 MILLION YEARS AGO

Australia lay close to the South Pole and had several months of winter darkness. Seas covered half the land. Pterosaurs or flying reptiles were common. *Kronosaurus queenslandicus* was the world's largest marine reptile at that time. Its skull was 4 m long!

Muttaburrasaurus langdoni
Source: Investigating Australian Geography and Citizenship, Sue Baker © 2001 Cengage Learning Australia Pty Limited. Reproduced with the permission of Cengage Learning Australia.

The bones of this dinosaur were found at Muttaburra in Queensland. They were amongst material deposited by an ancient sea. Its reconstructed skeleton makes it Australia's most complete dinosaur.

FRAME 5 – 15 MILLION YEARS AGO

Giant-sized animals or **megafauna** existed. They were the ancestors of our modern marsupials such as kangaroos and koalas. By 5 million years ago all our present day groups of marsupials were well established.

Known as *Mihirung*, this giant bird weighing 350 kg, lived until 26 000 years ago.
Source: Investigating Australian Geography and Citizenship, Sue Baker © 2001 Cengage Learning Australia Pty Limited. Reproduced with the permission of Cengage Learning Australia.

FRAME 6 – 200 000 YEARS AGO

Australia's climate became drier. Plants adapted to these conditions replaced inland rain forests. Animals had to adapt to water shortage. To take advantage of good seasons they had to be able to move and breed quickly like kangaroos do.

Diprotodons or giant wombat-like creatures, 3 m long and 2 m tall, were common. Their size was similar to that of the hippopotamus. They looked like a rhino without a horn. Weighing up to 2 800 kg, they were the largest marsupials ever known.

FRAME 7 – THE LAST 20 000 YEARS

The world was in the grip of an **Ice Age**. This was a period of cold temperatures when much of the water in the oceans froze up making sea levels lower. The Australian mainland was connected to Tasmania and New Guinea.

Most megafauna had died out by 15 000 years ago. By 10 000 years ago the Ice Age was coming to an end. The melting ice caused rising sea levels to flood the coastline. Tasmania was isolated as an island. The Australian mainland was cut off from New Guinea. Australia's current plant life began developing about 8 000 years ago. Sea levels reached their present height about 6 000 years ago.

THE DREAMING

Aboriginal tribes each have their own rich culture of art, song, dance and stories handed down over generations. These form part of Aboriginal culture known as **The Dreaming**. The Dreaming began when the world was created. Ancestors came out of the ground and walked across the land. Every feature of the landscape had to do with this journey. A red rock for example, may be where an ancestor stopped to spear a kangaroo and left its liver behind.

Ancestors shaped the land surface by singing it into creation. Each ancestor left a trail of words and music behind as they travelled. Their grand journeys are called Dreaming Tracks or Song Lines. All living things are said to stem directly from the ancestors.

The Rainbow Serpent was the ancestor of many tribes. See how it created mountains, rivers and valleys as it slithered over the land? Source: Investigating Australian Geography and Citizenship, Sue Baker © 2001 Cengage Learning Australia Pty Limited. Reproduced with the permission of Cengage Learning Australia.

FROGSVILLE WAS RAPT AGAIN

'Well I never!' everyone said, after the talks. They all wanted to come to The Pumpkin Patch to go spotlighting and see the animals. They wanted more, more, more.

'I hope none of our critters is endangered,' someone said.

'Well actually, our quoll is,' Granny replied. 'And the rufous bettong and eastern pygmy possum are vulnerable in NSW.'

'Then what can *we* do about all this endangered animal business?' a farmer asked.

'We could replant belts of trees to connect up to Granny's forest. Then the animals could move around more safely. And then the quolls might not come after our chickens,' another farmer said.

Over my dead body, not on my land Humph thought.

'What about building some nesting boxes?' someone else suggested. 'They could make up for all the trees with hollows that we've cut down. We should map out a plan to get rid of all the feral animals too.'

'I think all those ideas are brilliant,' the Mayor said. 'I think we should call it the Frogsville Wildlife Recovery Project. I will look into some government funding. When we have things underway we should encourage other communities to do the same. Now Humph, your farm is closest to Granny's. What say we start there and then fan out?'

'What a fabulous idea,' Granny said.

'Er well, er I spose so,' Humph replied. He was well and truly trapped, just like old foxy loxy. 'I could *kill* that bleedin' woman and her loony kids,' he whispered to Mavis.

Piles or no piles, Granny skipped and danced around for a whole week. Thankyou universe for turning things around for me, she said to herself every day. She was thrilled too, with the kids' detective work. She thought apart from Pete and Phant going Missing in Action that her *Grand Plan* was advancing beautifully. But would things be quite so rosy when the kids found themselves smack in the middle of crocodile-infested waters on their next case?

POBBLEBONK DETECTIVE ACTIVITY

- Compare the height and weight of a red kangaroo to yours to get an idea of their size.
- Check out the variety of kangaroos and their rellies at <rootourism.com.au>.
- Make a collage of unusual Australian animals or animals in your country.
- Create a collection of pictures to show what Australia and its environments look like today. Overseas Detectives could make a collection for their country.
- Collect a second set to show what your country looked like in the past.
- Find out what animals lived at different times.
- Explore the website <abc.net.au/science/ozfossils/megafauna>. Here you can play the Pitfall Game looking for hidden fossils on a cave floor. You can also explore the world of sea monsters.

CHAPTER 8: OLD MAN CROCODILE

Pete saw it in a dream.

'DEATH BY CROCODILE'

Pete's nightmare

'I d–d–don't want to go,' he stuttered. 'I d–d–don't want to be eaten by a croc. And I'm terrified of deep water and boats. You can't do things like this to little kids Granny.' Pete had nightmares of being caught in a croc's jaw.

Granny was having nightmares too, of children overboard and falling into crocodile jaws.

Not to mention Ozzie disgracing himself as usual. She was contracted to work on a cruise off the Kimberley coastline in Western Australia. But what should she do with the kids? How much trouble was she inviting if she took them along?

MEMORANDUM

DATE: 0300 hrs May 6th
SUBJECT: Major Test

You are to go north with Granny and develop a thorough profile of Saltwater Crocodiles (known in Australia as 'salties'). This will give you the necessary skills should we need your help in profiling a serial killer. But more to the point, a rogue croc is creating terror in the Prince Regent River right where Granny is going. Now the boat captain seems a nice bloke, but he's dead set on catching that croc. He's tired of the panic it's causing to his passengers. We are concerned that he's got the wrong croc in his sights. It's up to you to sort this out before the wrong croc is trapped. You must do lots of research on your subject first. Your brief is attached.

Horace Fitzwilliam

THE INVESTIGATION

- Define and investigate the features of reptiles.
- Examine the reasons why crocs are such expert killers. Investigate body structure, size and movement, teeth, jaws, sight and other senses.
- Describe a year in the life of a saltie. Are salties aggressive at particular times?

- Find out how crocs fit into the ecosystem in which they live. How are they adapted to it? What food do they prefer: dinghies and fishermen? Or are they child-chompers?
- Explore the threats that crocs face.
- Look for the croc that hangs around the mouth of the Prince Regent River. Observe it closely especially for signs of aggressive behaviour. Make a decision as to whether this is the rogue croc.

OH GRANDPA -- WHAT LOVELY TEETH YOU HAVE!

Pete took the photo below, risking his life in murky, croc-infested waters!

Actually the photo was taken through a glass screen at a wildlife park where the kids went for some initial croc investigations. Pete named the croc Algernon after his English grandfather.

'Imagine the size of the drill and gear you'd need for those teeth. But his teeth are cone-shaped. I thought they'd be sharp and pointed.'

'The teeth are built for holding and crushing prey rather than chewing it,' Granny explained. 'A croc crushes its prey further by tightening its jaw muscles.'

So what would happen if Algernon's teeth got all decayed or fell out or worn down?' Pete asked, chewing his nails.

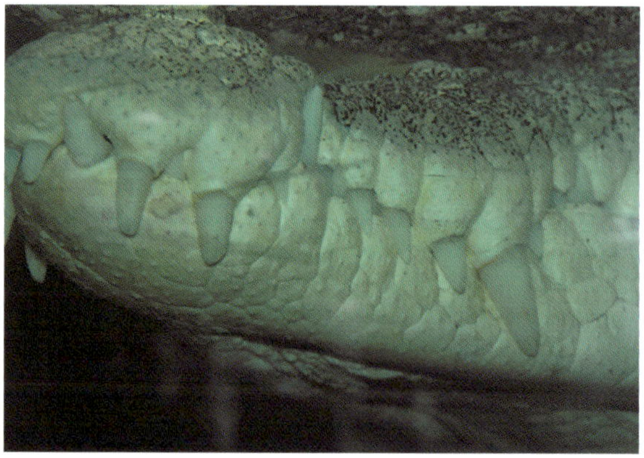

'I know Grandpa's teeth are long and stained, but surely his smile is not that bad! Ew! Imagine how that breath must stink. I bet it's worse than Ozzie's after he's eaten blue cheese,' Fee said.

'This guy sure needs a visit to the croco-dontist,' Ozzie joked.

'Sorry to make things worse for you Pete, but he's got a row of new teeth sitting waiting!' Granny said. 'The roots of his teeth are hollow cones into which replacements grow. But worse than that, a croc can replace 3 000 teeth in its lifetime!'

'Wow! This bloke is dead serious. Ain't nothin' gonna stop him from serial killing. Dya know how powerful a croc's bite is? It says here that it's seven times more powerful than that fearsome creature, the Great White Shark and five times stronger than a lion. It's got the strongest bite of any animal. Its force is like dropping a utility truck on your toe! Once those mighty jaws clamp down on you there ain't nuthin' that can prise them apart.'

Ozzie was enjoying winding Pete up. Pete turned away and bit his lip. But the killer profile got worse.

Nature's design masterpiece

- The lumps and bumps on the skin are called **scutes**. Each scute is placed to give maximum speed and skill in the water.
- The powerful tail and strong legs also make for fast movement.
- Notice how close together those eyes are? That isn't for cosmetic reasons! OMC has binocular vision! He can see things much larger and tell exactly where they are.

'A croc doesn't even need to see you in the first place!' Granny said. 'It has spots on the skin above its teeth. These sense changes in the water when something moves. No way you're going get away if he has you in his sights. And it's not just all these fancy features that make crocs expert killers, but they've had millions of years to develop and refine them.'

THE DEATH ROLL

Every killer has a unique **Modus Operandi** or method of operation. Old Man Croc's is a death roll. This is a kind of dance he does before killing. Once the victim is in his jaws, he rolls over and over. OMC just loves to 'crock and roll'. He learned this dance from watching TV. The victim becomes disoriented and drowns. OMC may even store the victim in his under-water pantry for a midnight snack!

PUMPKIN PATCH POST - REPTILES

Reptiles have dry, scaly skin - like Humph Ozzie thought. Only reptiles are more handsome! Watertight skin enables them to live on land. They are **vertebrates** with backbones and breathe through lungs. Most reptiles lay eggs. Some give birth to live young. They are mostly carnivores.

Mammals such as humans are **warm-blooded**. Their temperature is controlled within the body. But reptiles are **cold-blooded**. The *environment* determines their body temperature. They bask in the sun when they need to warm up and seek cover when they need to cool down.

Reptiles include **crocodilians** (crocs, alligators, caimans and gharials), lizards, snakes and turtles. Famous reptiles include Komodo Dragons, boa constrictors, taipans, iguanas and Gila Monsters. Apache Indians believed the breath of a Gila Monster could kill a person. Maybe it smells so bad because its mouth is also used as its anus!

Reptiles dominated the earth from 248 to 65 million years ago. This period is called **The Age of the Reptiles**. Giant lizards with flippers dominated the seas. The most awesome reptiles were the dinosaurs. An asteroid hitting the earth 65 million years ago caused a **mass extinction**, wiping out many species. But the ancestors of modern crocs survived. Nothing was going to hold *them* back.

A REPTILE YOU WOULDN'T WANT TO MEET - THE KOMODO DRAGON

Komodo Dragon

This is the world's largest lizard species. Growing 2-3 m long, it weighs up to 70 kg! Now here's the gruesome part. The teeth are covered with tissue that cuts easily, making an ideal place for deadly bacteria to grow. Any creature that is bitten dies a long, agonising death from blood poisoning. The dragon tracks down its victim later when it is dead. It can smell a dead or dying animal from 9.5 km away! Some people think these guys are so interesting that the national park in Indonesia in which they live is on the World Heritage List!

POBBLEBONK FACT SHEET **SUBJECT:** Saltwater or Estuarine Crocodile

SCIENTIFIC NAME: *Crocodylus porosus*
HABITAT: warmer tropical waters. River **estuaries** (the tidal part of a river nearest the sea) are perfect habitat. Some crocs venture 200 km or so up rivers. They like freshwater wetlands within 100 km of the sea too. Also found throughout South East Asia.
SIZE: largest of the world's thirteen croc species; world's largest reptile. Body length averages 4.2-4.8 m. Some males reach 7 m. The longest saltie listed in the Guinness Book of Records, measures 7.1 m. It lives in an Indian wildlife sanctuary.
WEIGHT: average 400-520 kg. Some are known to weigh over 1 000 kg.
GROWTH RINGS: crocs have growth rings in their bones. Wide rings indicate wet seasons when food was plentiful. Narrow rings indicate dry seasons.
LIFE SPAN: from the growth rings it is known that crocs live up to seventy years. A freshwater croc known as 'Mr Freshy' caught by the famous croc hunter Steve Irwin and his dad and taken to their zoo was reckoned to be 130. In the wild, the average male is mature at 3.3 m and sixteen years old. Some hang out to the big 100 to get congrats from the Queen!
DIET: small crocs - fish, crabs, prawns, small animals. Adults - larger prey including humans, pigs, cattle, sharks. Larger crocs can survive on one or two good meals a year.
HOMING INSTINCT: troublesome crocs are relocated. Some return to their home after being relocated up to 400 km away, sometimes in a matter of weeks. Then they usually end up at a croc farm.

CROC TRACKS: look like the mark left by a strange, wide tyre with footmarks.

MEETING SWEETHEART – A MAN-HATING CROC

Lying there so quietly, Algernon certainly didn't look like a serial killer Pete thought. So it was off then to find out about a croc that almost was. The gang headed to Darwin Museum to see its pride and joy – the skeleton of Sweetheart, a famous Northern Territory croc.

SWEETHEART'S VITAL STATISTICS
Weight: 780 kg
Length: 5.1 m
Maximum Girth (measurement around the body): 2.3 m
Age: About 50 years old

Local Aborigines knew him as Old Man Sweets Lookout, or Sweets for short. Sweets lived in a billabong on the Finniss River in the 1970s. Happy to have fishermen as company for years, something happened to change him. He viciously attacked so many boats that he became world famous. What made him so angry? Did someone try to shoot him or did he get an 'I Don't Love You Any More' letter from some girl croc? We will never know.

In his first attack, Sweets struck a dinghy shaking it about and tearing the metal. When the driver started up the motor to escape, Sweets grabbed onto the propeller and mangled it. Next he put four holes in a dinghy, wrecking the motor. He had a thing about motors. Did he think that maybe the noise was another creature invading his patch? Or had a propeller injured him at some time?

Locals dubbed the attacks 'The Sweetheart Embrace'. On occasions, Sweet's teeth missed fishermen by centimetres. He continued to terrorise that billabong until something just had to be done.

'Poke a rifle down its throat and give it both barrels,' someone advised. But Sweets wasn't having any of that and attacked the motor on the shooters' boat. Next, rangers tried to net him using dead crocs as bait, tape recordings of crocodile roars and even sonic equipment.

Finally it was decided to trap and relocate him. A trap was set using a dead dingo as the lure. Taking the bait, Sweets was caught in a noose, fighting and thrashing for a whole night. Next day he was sedated, roped up and towed across the river to a trailer. On the way he swallowed water into his lungs. His captors tried to siphon the water out. But it was too late – Sweets drowned.

Sweet's capture made world headlines. His body was exhibited around Australia.

THE DADDY OF THEM ALL!

'Look over here,' Ozzie yelled across the museum. 'It's a special croc exhibition! Look at the size of this! It's called *Sarcosuchus imperator*. '*Sarco*' means flesh, '*suchus*' means crocodile and '*imperator*' means emperor. Its fossil remains were found in Africa's Sahara Desert when it was a lush tropical area.'

Growing up to 12.2 m long, Sarco was almost the length of a bus! A third longer than a saltie, it weighed up to eight tonnes. That is eight times heavier than the largest living saltie. The 132 teeth of its huge jaw are described as being like railway spikes. Sarco had scutes the size of roof tiles. This provided an armour-like protection of its body. It lived during the Age of the Reptiles.

'Well,' Granny said, trying to soothe Pete's increasing anxiety. 'You wouldn't want to mess with one of those guys. Thank heavens they are extinct. Compared to him, there isn't much to worry about eh?'

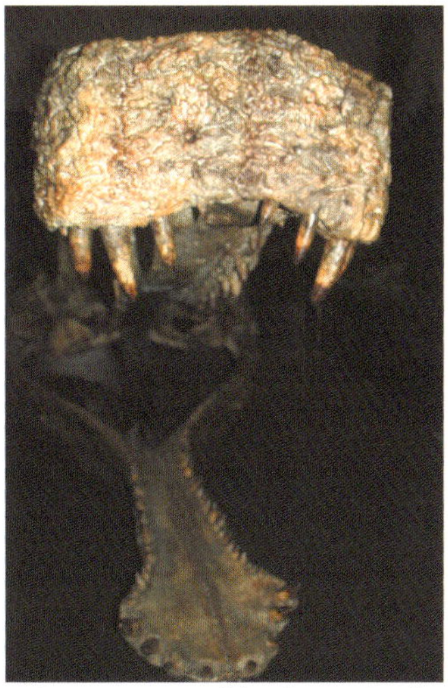

Ancient crocs like Sarco had heads as big as a human body!

A DISASTROUS START TO THE CRUISE

'It's so wild up here,' Pete complained. 'I could tread on a croc and not even know.'

It was time now to set off on the voyage to the wild and remote coastline between Darwin and Broome. At the last moment Pete demanded to be left on shore.

'Come on,' Granny pleaded. 'You will be perfectly safe. Besides, I need you to help me with my lectures. And with the tasks SHIDS have set, you'll be too busy to worry.'

First up was a fire and evacuation drill. Everyone had to don life jackets. None would fit around Ozzie's big tummy. The drill went on forever.

'Do you think maybe we're on the Titanic?' Pete asked, fumbling with the ties on his jacket. 'Do the crew know something we don't?' As it turned out, they did.

'Okay,' the captain said. 'First we must do a twenty-four hour crossing of the Joseph Bonaparte Gulf. A large open stretch of water, it is often rough.' It was rough all right.

A buffet dinner was served. Ozzie thought the seafood platter was the most delicious sight of all time. The swell picked up tossing the boat around. One by one the passengers retired to nurse their misery. But not Ozzie, he was determined to make it to dessert. By that time there were four dessert eaters and twenty-one deserters! The boat crashed down on a large swell making an enormous thwack. Ozzie's stomach flew up into his chest. He brought up his dinner, all over chef's prize sticky date pudding! As he slunk off, he begged the chef to make sure another seafood buffet was served the next day.

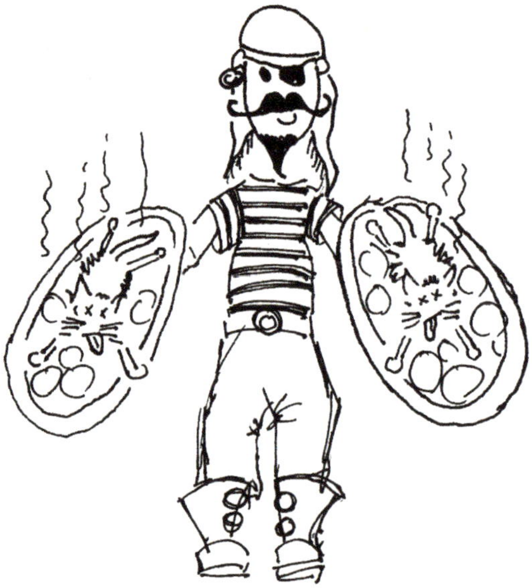

Huh, the chef thought. I'll fix you boy. I'll serve up something really gruesome. Throw a bit of sauce over it and you boy, would never stop to see the difference.
Cartoon by Sam Oakes

Ozzie gathered up the others and they headed upstairs to watch TV. The boat rode up each swell and thumped down. Bang, crash, thud, wham, whack. Then it rolled to one side then the other. It seemed that it would roll right over. One almighty bang brought the door off its hinges. Another, and the TV crashed off its mountings, smashing down centimetres from Pete.

'Let's go downstairs and find Granny,' he screamed. But now it was so rough that they had to crawl down the stairs then along the passageway, hanging on for dear life.

'Now you know why we call it Joseph *Blown Apart* Gulf,' Captain joked.

'It's no laughing matter,' Pete sobbed hysterically. 'You get me outta here. Get an emergency helichopper in if you have to. I don't care if I have to walk in the wild for six months to get to a town or half starve, just get me to land.' The boat's nurse gave Pete a pill to make him sleep.

Everyone gathered in the small lounge downstairs, the most stable part of the boat. They slept on the floor and lounge chairs. The next morning for those who could stomach it, the crew served tea and toast. At last the fearsome crossing was complete and the boat glided into calm water. Pete had never been so thankful.

THE STATUS OF SALTIES

Pete set up an office on the back deck as the boat headed for the Prince Regent River. Here he could admire the ancient, towering red cliffs and waterfalls that poured into the sea. Oh how I'd love to be safe on one of those tiny, lonely beaches he thought. But polishing up his work for Granny's lecture took his mind off things. Fee taught him how to pronounce the big words. Once he learned more about salties Pete began to change his opinion of them.

'If we had been here fifty years ago, we would be lucky to see many crocs,' he told the other passengers. 'You know, because they were hunted. People shot them for fun, sport, meat and those beautiful skins to make belts, shoes and handbags. The belly skin of salties is highly prized, because the scales are more even-sized than on other crocs.'

Croc numbers got so low that hunting was banned. Up to 25 000 may have been taken in Western Australia alone. Now, numbers are slowly rising and the population is healthy. That is important, as crocs are the big guys at the top of the food web. If they are removed, all other living things in their habitat will be affected. Some people think that without hunting, croc numbers will explode. That is not so because of their high **mortality** or death rate. Only 1% or so of eggs make it to young crocs. They are not so lucky in other parts of the world.

ENDANGERED MEMBERS OF THE WIDER CROCODILE FAMILY

Chinese Alligator: less than 130 remain, mainly because of draining wetlands for rice farms.
Siamese Crocodile: almost extinct in Thailand and Vietnam and only a small number in Laos mainly due to habitat loss and hunting. Largest remaining numbers are in Cambodia.
Philippine Crocodile: about 100 left of a once healthy population, due to habitat loss and hunting for skins.
Orinoco Crocodile: a South American crocodile heavily hunted for skin. Less than 250 remain in the wild.

ERIC TURNED UP

'Come quick,' Ozzie panted, rushing into the boat's lounge. 'The most humungous croc is lying in the water. I think it must be the one that SHIDS asked us to look out for.' Pete nervously eyed the croc through his binoculars. He reckoned it was 4 m long. The croc just floated, looking happy. His powerful hind legs were stretched out to keep him stable.

'I think he's gorgeous,' Ozzie said. 'I'm going to name him Eric. He seems to be lovin' our company and having something to watch. Must get boring at times I guess for a croc out here all on his own.'

The kids watched Eric during morning tea. His eyes moved slowly along the deck.

'He's looking for the best meal,' Ozzie laughed.

'Yeah, his big yella eyes always come back to you,' Pete said. Gutzing into a handful of lemon tarts, Ozzie's big belly was hanging over the rail. 'That's why his eyes and nostrils are higher than the rest of the head. He can still see you Ozzie, and also breathe at the same time without being too obvious.'

Then the croc swam slowly towards the boat. Pete observed how he tucked his feet into his sides.

'That gives him less water resistance,' Granny said. 'And his feet are webbed. That allows him to make fast turns and to walk in shallow water.'

'Where's he going? What *is* he gonna do?' Pete whispered, his heart hammering. 'Can he get us from here?'

'Just watch quietly,' Granny said. 'And keep your arms inside the railings.'

'Let's set a test. Throw some ropes off the back deck,' Captain said. 'Then we'll see if he tries to attack them.' Eric swam behind the back deck, and then suddenly leapt up.

'Oh,' everyone shrieked, drawing back. Please, Pete prayed, don't let him be aggro.

'Look at that, he's *playing* with the ropes!' Ozzie said, delighted. Lunging up, Eric did target practice, latching on and tugging. What a ball – something to play with! He was as gentle as a kitten playing with string. After a while he resumed his floating position, watching everything happening on the boat for the rest of the day.

'He thinks he's at the movies,' Ozzie laughed. 'Ya know he's just like a pet. I can't imagine *him* attacking boats.'

Later that day Pete overheard Captain on the radio.

'I think we've found that mongrel,' he said. 'When can you get a trapping team up here? Thirty-six hours? That's fantastic.'

'Captain, if this croc is the monster then how come he hasn't attacked our boat?' Pete asked.

'You wait and see. He's just waiting for the right moment.'

'What can we do?' Pete pleaded to Granny. 'We can't sit by and see an innocent animal punished for crimes it didn't do.'

'I agree. We haven't seen a single sign of aggression. Only thing we can do is go up the river and keep looking.'

THE MYSTERY OF THE RED LIGHTS

Granny had to drag Pete into the small explorer boat, the *Intrepid*.

'We could get macarooned out there on the low tide,' he wailed. 'We could die before anyone even found us. We haven't seen another person or even a house for a whole week! Did you see how that tide sucks out all the way to the horizon? And the way it races back in charging like a mad, angry surf is truly fearsome.'

The boat puttered up the Prince Regent River. Night kissed it with her ghostly blackness.

'Er, now folks,' Captain said. 'I know this isn't exactly on your itinerary. We always have a few croc-spotting trips at night. But um, this one's a bit different. You see I'm trying to track down that rogue croc that's been terrorising boats in this part of the river. This one's really crockers – every time we've been up here in the past two months he's had a go at us. It cost me a brand new motor last time. So I'm gonna find that mongrel come hell or high water. And then he's going in the crock-pot for a nice long stew.'

'Geez, you'll need a large bag of onions for that,' Ozzie laughed.

'Good heavens man, are you insane?' asked a man with large red cheeks. 'You're putting our lives at risk. Take us back at once!'

'Don't panic,' Captain said forcefully. 'Just keep all your body bits well in from the side of the boat.' He turned all the lights off and slowed the engine down so that it barely made a noise.

'Come up the front with me,' Granny said, as she saw Pete dive into the aisle and cover himself with a blanket. 'You can be our chief croc-spotter.'

'Are you crazy – how could you see a croc in this pitch black murk?'

Granny handed Pete a special torch, telling him to sweep the light along the banks. The eerie, twisted shapes of mangrove trees rose up from the mud. Sucking in his breath, Pete drew his lanky arms and legs tightly in to his body and huddled up against Granny.

'What if we tip over? What if that rogue croc lunges at our boat? These crocs are not known as leg-trimmers for nothing,' he whispered.

Struggling to hold the torch steady, Pete finally managed to focus on a far bank. What was that? Everyone craned forward. A pair of small sinister-looking red lights glowed brightly. Peering over the rims of his bifocals the captain's little black button eyes had trouble seeing where to steer without navigation lights. With strange hand signals from Granny to show him where to go, the *Intrepid* crept towards the mud bank.

Pete could almost imagine the croc in the day-time, sun-baking and sipping a cocktail!

The boat inched way too far onto the bank as far as Pete was concerned. The tide was falling. What if the boat got stuck high and dry? The red lights were close now. It was a croc! Would it be the rogue? Pete waited for it to start thrashing and lunging. But it just lied quietly catching prawns and small fish! It wasn't a monster at all.

'Is it a male or female?' Ozzie asked.

'Only one way to tell,' Captain said. 'Flip it over and see!'

'How come its eyes glow red in the night?' Pete asked.

Granny explained that like many other animals, behind its eye is a layer of crystals that reflect light back onto the retina. When light is shone on the eyes the crystals give a red shine. All the better to see you with my dears!

This wasn't scary at all. Pete looked keenly for more eye-shine. As the Intrepid glided on, he found another pair of red eyes. This croc was a whopper, about 4 m. Lying asleep, its mouth was wide open to keep cool. All those gruesome teeth showed like a row of super-sharp white fence posts. This croc didn't open an eye either, didn't budge. Where was all the action? It was becoming clear that although you can *never* trust a crocodile they are not always aggro.

COULD THE ROGUE CROC BE HUNGRY?

'Do you think maybe the rogue croc is aggro because he's hungry?' Fee asked.

'Absolutely not,' Granny replied. 'Mangroves are one of the earth's richest habitats. Crocs love living here because food is so plentiful. I'll explain.'

Mangroves are trees that grow in soft, muddy soils along coastlines, rivers and bays. Often surrounded by large mudflats they are favourite saltie habitat.

Mangroves might look boring, but they are one of the earth's richest habitats because:

- The leaves that they shed are broken down by bacteria. This creates a protein-rich food for many creatures. Crabs really like to snack on the broken down leaves.
- Tides wash billions of food particles in and out each day.
- The tangled tree roots plus shallow water and plenty of food, make a perfect place for baby fish and prawns to shelter and feed. These provide food for many other creatures. And those creatures in turn are food for even bigger creatures.

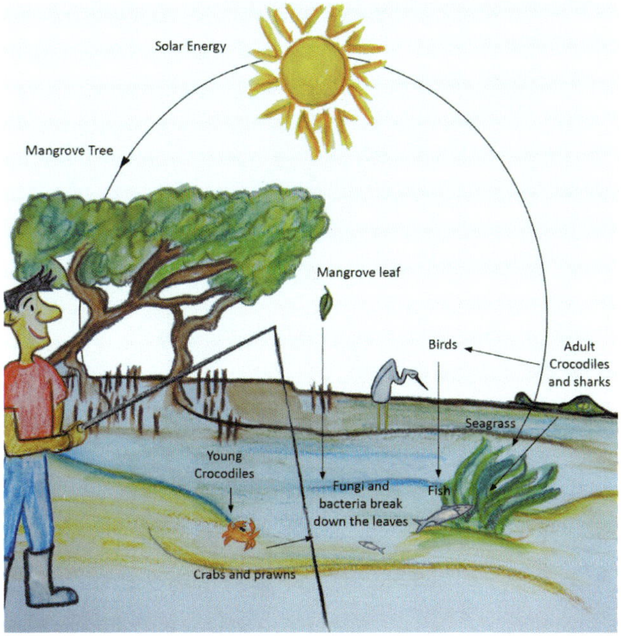

Mangrove food web

A YEAR IN THE LIFE OF A SALTIE

'Okay then food is not the problem,' Fee said. 'So let's take a look at the croc's yearly cycle. You know, maybe the rogue croc is aggro because it's mating season or something.' Once again the kids got hard to work and Ozzie shared their findings with the other passengers. He was still trying to make amends for the ruined sticky date pudding.

- A croc becomes sexually active when the wet season begins in late October. OMC isn't faithful. Patrolling a 20 km river stretch, his harem may have twenty girls. Unfaithful as well, the girls store the sperm of several males. Those babies must have an identity crisis – nobody knows whose father is who! And what would be written on their birth certificates?

- Females take up to two weeks to build a nest – a mound of soil and plant matter. An average of fifty eggs is laid in an hour. Now you wouldn't want to be around then because the protective sheilas hang round the nest for eighty days or so and are most aggro.

- Nest temperature decides whether hatchlings are male or female. At around 31.6°C mainly males will be produced; a little higher or lower and females will result.

Unbelievable eh, that such a cute creature grows up to be such a monster?
Fee reckoned that's what everyone thinks about Ozzie.

- Hatchlings chew at their shell with a tiny tooth. Calling from inside the egg, they let Mum know it is time to dig up them up and carry them to the water. She does this in a soft pouch in her lower jaw. Too bad if she gets a fright and chomps down eh? She might even carefully roll the unopened eggs between her jaws to help the hatchlings out. On average they weigh a tiny 72 grams and are 29 cm long. The young are kept in nurseries for eight weeks or until they can look after themselves.
- Lying on the banks with open mouths, a saltie basks in the sun during the cooler months. The sun heats the exposed fleshy tongue and the warmed blood flows to the body organs. Heartbeat slows down and less food is eaten. OMC needs a rest now and stops frisking around with the girls.

THE CLOCK TICKED ON

Everyone agreed there was nothing in Ozzie's info that could explain the rogue croc's more than normal aggression. Time was ticking by. Eric still floated peacefully by the boat and made no attacks. By now all the passengers had fallen in love with him and were desperate to save him. So, frightened as they were, they urged Captain to take them up the river again that night. It was the same scene as before – crocs lying asleep or quietly feeding. Not a sign of action anywhere.

'It just has to be that mongrel Eric back at the boat,' Captain said. Pete looked around and saw everyone's looks of despair.

The wind had picked up, creating a swell. The *Intrepid* strained its way back. Captain had to manoeuvre it alongside the rear of the mother ship. But now the little boat rocked and rolled wildly in the choppy water. A number of red lights hovered nearby. And suddenly one pair of those wicked lights came full force towards the Intrepid. Everyone screamed, jumping into the aisle. The Intrepid rocked even more wildly.

'Sit down,' Captain roared. At that same instant a jaw full of giant teeth lunged out of the water trying to attack the motor at the rear. *Please* don't let it be Eric, Pete prayed.

'Quick Ozzie,' a crew member screamed urgently from the upper deck. 'You're the closest. Throw the rope up so we can tie the boat up and get you all off.' Ozzie grabbed the rope and threw it with all his might. But it landed, plop back into the river. A cry of dismay went up in unison – how useless could you be Ozzie? The little boat bobbed around in the murk with red lights circling everywhere. And then up came the croc again, the most frightening sight the kids had ever seen. But this time the croc sunk its teeth into the hull. And as it sunk back into the water it created a wave that rocked the boat even more.

Now it was do or die. Granny took over the steering wheel while Captain raced forward to retrieve the rope. He hurled it upwards, the crew grabbed it and the *Intrepid* was tied alongside. As the shaking passengers alighted from the boat the monster rose up again.

'Did you see *that*?' Pete cried. 'It's got a huge, gruesome injury underneath its throat. It *can't* be Eric.'

'Eric's still over there, exactly where he was when you went out,' Chef said. 'That other guy has probably been in a fight with a shark. No wonder he's been so aggro.'

The monster lunged out of the water yet again. One almighty swish of his tail and Eric headed for it. He struck out at the rogue with his jaw. The water boiled as they thrashed and snapped at each other. As the rogue began to withdraw, Eric chased him off.

'I've never seen anything like that in my entire sea-going life,' Captain said.

The trapping team arrived next morning and went off to see what they could do for the injured croc. It was time to leave Eric who was still floating quietly by the boat.

'He's gonna be so lonely and miserable,' Pete sobbed. 'I feel dreadful leaving him. It's like walking away from Phant.'

WOULD PETE BE A LION TAMER NOW?

'Wow,' Pete said to Granny. 'How brave have I been?'

'Wait till you get home and tell everyone you're an expert croc-spotter,' Granny said. 'See, I told you could do *anything*. And you've just proved me right. All you have to do is confront your fears.'

What a long way I've come since arriving at The Pumpkin Patch, he thought proudly. He dreamt of being a lion tamer and swimming with sharks. But his dreams didn't last long. A most urgent case was waiting on the family's return home. Concerning an indelicate subject, it would bring fame (some good, some bad) to the kids – and utter disgrace to Granny.

POBBLEBONK DETECTIVE ACTIVITY - REPTILE SCIENCE

- Carry out an Internet search - 'saltwater crocodile + death roll' - to find web sites where the death roll is shown.
- Find a copy of *The Saga of Sweetheart* by Col Stringer and read the full story of this croc.
- See how salties are hunted and trapped at <crocodilehunter.com.au>.
- Make a list of all the croc's adaptations e.g. for swimming, seeing, hearing and catching prey.
- Find out what reptiles might live in your local area.
- The Gila Monster starred in a movie, *The Giant Gila Monster*. Does it deserve this name and its fearsome reputation? A sausage-shaped **venomous** or poisonous lizard, it grows only to 60 cm. Why then do people regard it as a monster? Why has it been given legal protection? Where does it live?
- Pete reckons the Komodo Dragon is scarier than a croc. It is worth some detective work just to find out about its amazing table manners!
- Search for video clips showing Komodo Dragons and Gila Monsters.
- Add at least eight new words to your Earth Detective Dictionary.

CHAPTER 9: POO DUN THE BREAK-IN?

MEMORANDUM

DATE: 0600 hrs May 20th **SUBJECT:** Humphrey!

Get over to Humphrey's place urgently! He is laid up in bed with the flu. Mavis found rat poo all over her kitchen. Humphrey has told her to spread rat poison *everywhere*. Get your skills to work and find out poo dunnit. It could be the work of an innocent native rodent. Your brief is attached.

Horace A. Fitzwilliam

THE INVESTIGATION

- Build a profile of the suspected criminal. Identify the features that class rats and other animals as rodents.
- Define a rat.
- Compare the appearance, scats, burrows and habitats of native rats and mice at Frogsville and the introduced Black Rat, Brown Rat and House Mouse.
- Narrow the list of suspects by researching other small native animals that could be mistaken for rats.
- Convince Humphrey that native rats and mice are harmless and clean, unlike introduced black and brown rats.

Thanks Humph, the party was great.

THE CASE UNFOLDED

Ozzie groaned, 'geez don't we detectives ever get a break? Better get busy I spose. I couldn't bear the idea of going back to Earth Ignoramus status. What would we do then? Watch the pumpkins grow?' Ozzie rang Mavis.

'Don't touch a thing. We don't want the crime scene contaminated. We'll just bone up a bit on rats as fast as we can and we'll be right over to help.'

Horace's memo was one problem but what about Ozzie's long-wished-for date with Samantha? At last he was to take her out, to the school dance on his birthday. Fee had given him his present three weeks ago – deodorant, breath freshener, toenail clippers, shampoo and Clearasil for the zits. She wrote instructions of what to use, when and how. The outcome remained to be seen but meanwhile it was on with the case.

The kids hung up a sign on the front fence and headed off to Humph's.

AT YOUR SERVICE – BUFO'S PEST CONTROL EXPERT SCATOLOGISTS AND RAT TRACKERS C/- THE PUMPKIN PATCH

'Surely our prime suspect must be *Rattus rattus,* the dreaded Black Rat? See, the gnaw marks are unmistakably those of a rodent,' Ozzie told a tearful Mavis. He collected the scats from amongst the chewed apples. 'Some party they had eh?'

'Remember, the first rule of detective work is to keep an open mind. Do not convict until firm evidence is available,' Pete said. 'Before any action is taken we need to find out what is around in the way of native rats and mice.'

'Str..ewth Humph,' Ozzie said. 'What happened to you? Why does your mouth look so peculiar?' He stared at the almost non-existent lips and the sunken cheeks.

'I lost me false teeth last night. Mavis has searched everywhere,' he hacked and snorted from his sick bed. Whoa! Stand clear!

'What a load of rubbish I heard you tell Mavis. Native animals my foot, they're all vermin, all pests, filthy, stinking, disease-ridden things. Just put out a whole lot of bait and poison the bleeding lot.'

'No way,' Fee exploded. 'Firstly, we might kill harmless native animals, all of which play important roles in the ecosystem. Secondly, rat poison causes agony for *any* creature that eats it. And that includes the rats themselves. It ruptures their blood vessels, causing internal bleeding. Their agony may go on for days. During this time and after, the rat can be easy prey for wildlife, and our pets. And then those creatures are poisoned too and whatever eats them as well.'

'Rats are important food for owls. Both our owl species up here are already under threat. It is far better to use traps than poison for *any* rodent. But make sure it is a safe trap that won't hurt the animal, or you.'

But Humph was still not convinced. Meanwhile Pete got on the Internet, discovering something wonderful. There is no longer a need to use horrible traps and dispose of their even more horrible contents! Now you can buy a device that plugs into a power point. It emits electromagnetic waves and sounds that drive mice and rats away!

ANYONE FOR *RATTUS RATTUS* DIP?

'Dya know,' Ozzie told Humph the next day, 'that some people actually value rats? In Ghana, that's an African country if you don't know, Cane Rats are bred as a major protein source. Stewed with tomatoes, chilli, pepper and salt, they are served with rice. In fact half Ghana's local meat is rats and mice. Mouse meat is a Chinese delicacy. Granny was once invited to dinner in a remote Thailand village. Rats were served all neatly lined up on a platter still wearing their fur coats and tails!'

Humph's face was creased in utmost disgust. The big eyebrows nearly burst right off his forehead. Fee decided to wind him up further. She was so overjoyed she no longer cared what she said to anybody. You see, she had toiled so hard to prove herself to old IRK. And guess what? She beat Samantha in the last exams by ten marks! And more than that, Frogsville came second in the state Geography Competition. Everyone was thrilled.

'Apparently rat meat is tender, sweet and tastes like frogs' legs. You see Humph it's all a matter of taste. Anyway we are thinking of serving rats at our next barbecue.'

'Pete is checking out recipes for rat dip! Personally I'd like to make a rat dessert. Ozzie wants to stuff them. You are most welcome to come.' If Humph wasn't sick before he certainly was now.

'Really Humph have you ever thought about how much we owe to rats? Being so clever and adjusting well to new situations, they are widely used in medical and scientific research. Think about all the drugs, diets and effects of diseases that are tested on them. Where would we be without them?' Ozzie said. Pete pulled out a book.

'Look in here. I bet you didn't know that Australia has a whole mob of native rats and mice. There's even a native Brush-tailed Rabbit-Rat and a Giant White-tailed Rat. They sound like characters out of a fantasy. Not to mention the Flat-skulled Marsupial Mouse!'

'Well I never!' said Mavis. 'Why don't we leave it to the kids then to sort this out?'

PUMPKIN PATCH POST - THE LOW-DOWN ON RODENTS

Rats are **mammals**. Like humans, they give birth to live young which **suckle** or drink milk from the mother. But rats and their relatives are also classed as rodents. **Rodents** have cute chisel-shaped incisor teeth at the front of their mouths, an adaptation for gnawing. Their teeth grow continually so they can keep gnawing away, making a nuisance of themselves. Australia has over fifty species of rodents.

A **rat** is any long-tailed rodent larger than a mouse. The world's best-known rats are the disease-carrying Black Rat - *Rattus rattus* (roof or ship rat) and the Brown Rat - *Rattus norvegicus* (sewer rat). Both were stowaways on ships to Australia. Pet rats are mostly Brown Rats that are bred from 'research' rats. But really they are the same as the rats found in any city sewer. The Black Rat is rather like the Cane Toad. It has displaced native rats especially the Bush Rat. An expert climber, it likes to feed on the eggs of native birds.

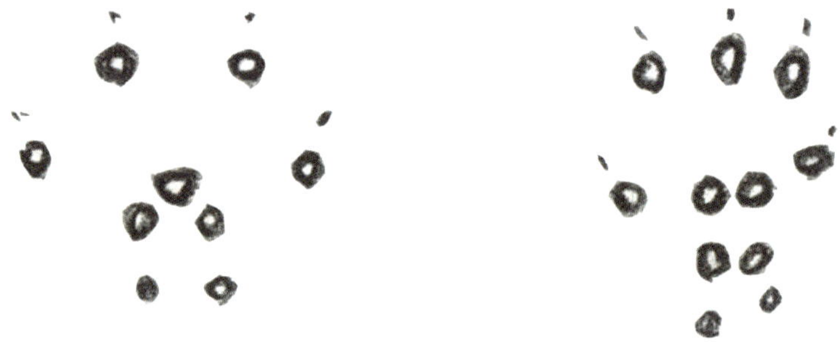

Typical Australian native rat footprints - front on the left, hind on the right.

POBBLEBONK DETECTIVE ACTIVITY - FANCY FOOTWORK

Okay Detectives, some footwork! All rodents have the same foot structure. This makes their tracks easy to pick out from those of other animals. Look at the drawing above. How many toes, claws and toe pads are on the front foot and hind foot?

FEE WAS CONCERNED ABOUT CATCHING THE BLACK DEATH

Something had troubled Fee ever since all this started. Back at home she looked through the well-worn pages of her health and hygiene book.

'Do you know that rats carry thirty-four diseases!' she exploded. 'And that Black Rats were responsible for the deaths of millions of people in Europe and other parts of the world?'

'Are we in danger?' Pete asked, thinking he couldn't take much more drama.

'The book calls it the 'Black Death' because people broke out in black spots, dying within three days. So many people died that it became known as the 'Black Plague'. In England over one quarter of the people died. Whole villages died out, abandoned forever. Some starved because so many farm workers died. All because of rats.'

'Ah, get with it,' Ozzie scolded. 'That was six centuries ago. Look what else your book says. In those days, garbage and human waste were thrown into the streets and people were crammed into small spaces. Medicines and antiseptics weren't invented then.'

'Ew,' Pete said through pursed lips. 'Look how you catch it.'

Rats thrived in the filth. High birth rates of twelve per litter were born as often as every three weeks. Young rats were ready to breed at ten weeks old. Rat numbers went crazy.

↓

Rats' blood contained deadly bacteria

↓

Fleas drank the rats' blood (now these were special fleas if you please: Oriental Rat Fleas!)

↓

The multiplying bacteria flooded the fleas' guts

↓

When the fleas bit a human, the rats' blood and bacteria regurgitated from their stomachs back into their mouths and into the bite.

THE TRAPS WERE SET

An urgent request was made for Granny's help. How can we track down the crims, the kids puzzled?

'We'd best use Elliot traps,' she advised, going to the shed. 'See – small mammals can crawl in through the doorway but can't get back out. This way they can be trapped and examined without being harmed. It's the smell that attracts them,' Granny said placing bacon rind, peanut butter and honey inside. That night, the first suspect was captured in Humph's garden.

'Look what we caught,' Pete yelled, running into Humph's room next morning. 'It's so gorgeous. Look at the cute pointed nose, long whiskers and the chisel-like teeth. And see how the hind feet stick out sideways! It doesn't even smell or look dirty. Go on Humph, feel the bristly fur.' Humph took the animal in his hand. It sat quietly, whiskers twitching, its tiny eyes gazing lovingly up at him. He was enchanted!

Pete tracked down the 'rat' in a book. It was actually a creature called an Antechinus (Anti-ky-nus), also known as a Broad-footed Marsupial Mouse.

Now Humph was really convinced to lay off the baits. Over the coming days the kids caught a variety of creatures. Weighed and measured, their physical features and tracks were photographed for the expanding Detective Files. Then the suspects were remanded in custody. Of course those precious calling cards were carefully examined too. It was the trap in the kitchen though that the kids were really sweating on results from.

PUMPKIN PATCH POST - SOS! THE ANTECHINUS

The Yellow-footed Antechinus.
'Hey, we're *not* house mice or rats!'
Reproduced by Permission of Oxford University Press Australia and New Zealand from a Field Guide to Mammals of Australia by Peter Menkhorst and Frank Knight © 2001 Frank Knight

Many types of Antechinus live in Australia. The name comes from Greek words, 'Anti' (resembling) and 'Echinos' (a sea urchin or hedgehog) - resembling a hedgehog. This refers to its bristly fur.

Because of their flat heads they have the funny common name of Flat-skulled Marsupial Mice. Four rows of small, sharp triangular-shaped incisors set them apart from the two chisel-shaped incisors of introduced rats and the house mouse. So too do the large, thin, crinkly ears.

Antechinus are creatures of the bush and are nocturnal insect eaters. Their scats are strong smelling cylinders of feathers or fur, or insect remains for smaller species.

In the bush they mostly live in tree hollows, coming down to the ground to **forage** or search for food. But they may make a comfy nest inside armchairs, old unused handbags, clothes drawers and old television sets. So farm kids, take care. Know what you are dealing with!

Now here is the interesting bit. Driven by changes in daylight length, all the males in a population go into a mating frenzy at the same time. It gets quite violent. Then 70% of the girls may give birth on the same day. Imagine the over crowding in the labour ward! But the poor males die about two weeks after mating. All that frenzied activity causes a break down in their immune system.

THE MOST LIKELY SUSPECT WAS CAUGHT

At last a creature was caught in the kitchen trap. Ozzie opened it up.

'Uh huh! Just as I thought – *Rattus rattus*. Constable, take the suspect to Interview Room 1. Let the videotape show that the interview commenced at 8.30 am.'

'Rattus where were you on the night of May 20th?'

'No comment.'

'Don't give me no comment. I'll have you shipped off to Siberia immediately.' It didn't take long for Rattus to crack.

'I was at home,' the rat whispered, quivering in fright.

'Speak up for the benefit of the recorder. And tell me – can anybody alibi that?'

'No,' Rattus said.

'Show me your teeth. Heavens, hasn't anyone told you about dental floss? Now bite into this apple so I have an impression of your teeth.'

'Where do you live? Come on, speak up.'

'My home is in the roof of Granny's shed, eastern end.'

'Constable, organise a search warrant for those premises.'

'Rattus, you are remanded in custody, pending further enquiries. Do not bother applying for bail.'

The children then began comparing the bite impression with the original apple that had been kept frozen. It looked close, but the left incisor was slightly crooked.

Pete scampered up the ladder into the shed roof.

'Holy hell, you should see what's up here,' he yelled down. 'It's a mess of rag and scraps, grass, bark and all sorts of paper. And the stink is something else. But you won't believe this,' he said, as he made his way down the ladder. In his hand was a heap of dental plates. One pair was monstrous and covered in black.

'Good evans, I think we've found Humph's missing falsies! Have you ever seen anything so gross?' Ozzie laughed.

'Rattus, what is the meaning of all these dentures?' Ozzie asked, as Rattus was reinterviewed.

'It's a way of not being caught,' Rattus replied. 'We use falsies to disguise our bite marks.'

'So where do all these dentures come from then?'

'I – I stole them from other rats, so that I had plenty of disguises. And the big human ones, well I took them because I'd never seen anything like it. I think it's time I had a lawyer.'

'You're out of luck, pal. All lawyers are at a conference this week.' Ozzie remanded Rattus back into custody along with the other suspects.

OZZIE'S ROOM *WAS* A RAT HOLE!

Racing into the office next morning, Ozzie yelled, 'come and look at this. I was out watching some cockatoos through my binoculars up near Humph's fence. You'll never guess what! Humph is out of bed and sittin' on the veranda. Mavis is plucking his nose hairs!' That afternoon Humph and Mavis came to check on the case progress.

'Something is different about you Humph,' Ozzie said. 'Your nose, what have you done to it?' Humph's face turned brick red.

'Look what I just found under Ozzie's bed,' Pete said, shrieking with glee as he danced onto the veranda. But Humph had arrived right at the worst possible moment. Just when the kids got on his good side, things went wrong again.

'What on earth is it?' Mavis said pointing to a mess in a cardboard box turned on its side. 'Oh,' she screeched, jumping back. 'It's a dead rat *and* its nest. How foul! Look at the withered, shrunken body.'

'Your room *is* a filthy rat-hole. I told you months ago about that awful stink,' Fee scolded. Humph and Mavis exchanged looks of utter disgust.

'Let's go and make that phone call. It's well overdue.'

PUMPKIN PATCH POST - MARSUPIAL RATS AND MICE

Most people who see something small and furry react with panic and assume it is a nasty rat. In this way, many harmless native creatures are killed with baits and poison. At least six native mice and four rat species are already extinct.

Few people know how to tell small, furry creatures apart. Even fewer know that Australia has a number of native *marsupial* rats and mice. Because some native rodents are called rats, people associate them with the illegal immigrants, the black and brown rats, the ones most commonly seen.

But unlike these pest rats, native species tend to steer clear of people. They don't build nests in roofs like the bad guys. Their nests are mostly built in dense undergrowth or in burrows under logs or rocks. And basically they're clean creatures - far more fussy in the bathroom than Ozzie! Only rats that live in dirty places like sewers and garbage dumps have a personal hygiene problem.

Native rats are usually dark brown with a whitish belly. Most species are nocturnal. They escape the heat of the day in burrows and are active at night. Their diet is mostly insects and other small prey.

Even possums can be mistaken for rats, especially if they're in a roof.

How are possums told apart from rats? Is the tail long, with a white tip and furry on the upper surface? Is it used to grip branches or held with the end slightly curled? Hey Guys! This one is a Ring-tailed Possum! Yes an adult may be the same size as a rat but look for that tail. Is the tail brushy? This can be a Brush-tailed Possum, Wambenger or Phasgocale (see Chapter 7).

Two books found in most libraries give a great run down on native rats and mice. One is *A Field Guide to the Mammals of Australia* by P. Menkhorst and F. Knight (published by Oxford University Press). The second is *Key Guide: Australian Mammals* by L. Cronin (published by Envirobook).

Here's a great website for info on native rats and lots of other interesting plants and animals – <abc.net.au/science/indepth/scribblygum>. Another one is <australianmuseum.net.au/is-it-a-rat>.

OTHER RAT LOOK-ALIKES

Dunnarts or Narrow-footed Marsupial Mice are mostly the size of house mice. And to the ignorant, that is what they could be mistaken for.

Reproduced by Permission of Oxford University Press Australia and New Zealand from a Field Guide to Mammals of Australia by Peter Menkhorst and Frank Knight © 2001 Frank Knight

Some dunnarts have distinct tails that become fat and carrot-shaped in good seasons. Living in dry country, their tails store fat as food reserves for poor times.

A BIG STINK AT THE PUMPKIN PATCH!

Meanwhile a dreadful stink came from the kitchen and Granny just couldn't track down the source. It was something dead under the house she thought. And Prim, her publisher had just phoned. She had something *most* important to discuss she said and wanted to call in. Granny was over the moon – she likes my new book she thought.

Ozzie's impersonation of IRK.

Ozzie was immediately despatched to the bathroom. Granny put in a frantic call to the pest control bloke, pleading come *urgently*. After crawling under the house, he was down on his knees on the kitchen floor. At that precise moment Prim arrived. Ozzie appeared from the bathroom dressed in a purple wig and gear, dying to do his impersonation of IRK for the visitor.

'This is the source of your smell,' the pest bloke said. He held up a plastic bag that he had found at the bottom of the broom cupboard. 'It's some sort of highly decomposed, revolting animal scat. How on earth would it get there?' he asked with alarm. 'Is it true then, the rumours I heard that the kids are playing with you-know-what?'

'Oh,' Pete said, full of joy. 'Thank you! I couldn't remember where I put that fox scat. Here Prim, have a look and a smell, then we'll tell you all about the exciting time we've had.' Prim shrunk back. What *was* this? And then – the Council Health Inspector appeared at the door. Talk about one disaster after another.

'Ah,' he said, looking embarrassed. 'We've – uh – had a report – um – that some children here might be living in unclean conditions or doing unclean things. I have an order to inspect the house.'

'Haven't you heard?' Fee said. 'We've been solving Poo Dunnit cases. And solve them we did.'

'You know, I'm writing about animal scats and how to use them for tracking,' Granny said. 'The kids are learning my tools of trade too. It's fine truly, I promise you. But sure, take a look around.' Granny shuffled stiffly to the sink to fill the kettle.

'Have you got arthritis?' Prim asked.

'No she's just got piles in her retina,' Pete said.

'Retina? That's in your eye. I think you mean rectum.'

'Oh my goodness. Is that why the doctor looked in her eye? I went in first you see. I was due for a testiness needle. I said to the doctor, I do hope you can do something about Granny's retina. She's in awful pain. I meant her piles and constipation. Wow can you really see it all from there I asked when he looked in Granny's eye!'

'Yes, well that's what I've come to discuss. It seems half the publishing world knows about your piles Granny, complete with vivid details. You've made our company a laughing stock. Have you seen what the children put on Facebook about you? It went out to all the email addresses on your computer. In fact, it went viral.'

'Oh you stupid, stupid children. You didn't.......' She switched on the computer and here was what Pete had written all that time ago:

OUR GRANNY

Our granny is great. She's had all sorts of adventures, like camping with lions and hippies. She knows all about the world and has tort us so mutch. She's a world famous writer too. We've had lots of fun up here at Frogsville - that is on Granny's good days. Her bad days are something else. Like today, she's dark, real dark. That's because she's got piles of piles, you know in her retina. Some days it really hurts when she moves around. Those are the days we think she'll send us off to Siberia.

And so the Facebook entry went on. Pete had added some gruesome pictures of piles that he found on the Internet. Granny couldn't bear to read it any further. Saying she had urgent business in Sydney, Prim marched off, looking like a stunned mullet.

SIBERIA?

At school the next day, Fee heard the story of the health inspector's visit being leaked by his son.

'Dad said Ozzie, all dressed up in a wig and womens' clothes was dancing around. Fee, tarted up in a tiara was pretending to be a Russian Princess, practising for a TV cooking show. Pete was feeding a cockroach in a house on the kitchen table. *At* the kitchen table sat a dog that dropped foul smells, one after the other. Pete was excited about some old fox poo that had stunk the house out. But the house was spotless, except for Ozzie's room, so Dad couldn't say the kids were neglected.'

The damage was done though. Once again there were smirks and whispers. Everyone gave the kids a wide berth. Word got round that the The Pumpkin Patch kids were playing with rats and rat poo. Some mothers threatened to withdraw their kids from the school if the gang wasn't expelled. But worst of all was the letter Granny received. She walked around all day crying, sniffling and muttering between clenched teeth.

Dear Granny,

I regret to inform you that we do not have the funds to publish your book at the moment. You might like to try some other publisher.

Yours sincerely,

Primrose Marsh

'What is Granny so busy doing on the Internet?' Pete asked.

'She's checking airfares to Siberia,' Fee said. 'Honestly do neither of you boys have *any* idea how to behave?'

That night Granny made a call to her daughter.

'Please, is there any way you can take the kids back. They have ruined my career. I can't take much more.' The children's mother cried. She just couldn't manage it.

THE COURT CASE

Judge Fee heads the trial

Meanwhile the possible rat suspects had been narrowed down to six. Another dreary, wet day came. So the detectives decided to sort out their suspects by setting up The Pobblebonk Courtroom. Judge Fee headed it.

'The rodents found at Pumpkin Patch are common in many parts of Australia. All Earth Detectives should know the difference between the scats and appearance of native rats and the passport-less introduced rats. So first I want a thorough run-down on the identikit of the suspects and their 'calling cards'. I want the suspects lined up as well. Now what's this HB business I see here in my notes? And tell me again, what is a 'naked' tail?'

'HB stands for head-body length Your Honda,' Pete, the clerk of the court replied. 'And a naked tail has no hairs.'

'And have you assembled all the evidence? Are the main witnesses present?'

'Yes your Honda. We're ready to proceed.'

IDENTIKIT 1

Scat: small, narrow, dark cylinders about 12 mm long.
Appearance: thin pointed ears. Chisel-like teeth leave obvious pairs of gnaw marks as evidence. Long and pointed head, HB 160-200 mm. Shiny fur, mostly mid-brown above, cream to white below. Upper parts of feet whitish.
Tail: clearly longer than body, thin, curves around, pinkish, naked with overlapping scales.
Habitat and Nest: lives around people and where there is plenty of rubbish to feed on. Especially likes grain stores. Nest of grass, bark, rags and paper in walls, ceilings, barns, tree hollows.
= *Rattus rattus*: Introduced Black Rat aka Ship's Rat

Black rat

Scat

Reproduced by Permission of Oxford University Press Australia and New Zealand from a Field Guide to Mammals of Australia by Peter Menkhorst and Frank Knight © 2001 Frank Knight

IDENTIKIT 2

Scat: larger, fatter than the black rat, like small sausages to 18 mm.
Appearance: small ears and eyes. Blunt nose. Upper feet pink. Dark brown body above, darkest on crown of the head. White to grey below. Detectives please note – this rat looks like the native Swamp Rat. Both have shaggy brown fur but the Swamp Rat's is greyish-tipped. HB 180-270 mm. May weigh twice as much as the Black Rat.
Tail: clearly shorter than body, tapers to a point at the end, grey-brown, naked, overlapping rings of scales.
Habitat and nest: around people. Lives on every continent except Antarctica. Some say it is the most successful animal on the planet after humans. Loves garbage dumps, flourmills and warehouses. Builds deep burrows with

front doors up to 10 cm wide in creek banks and drains. Nests also under floors or in empty rabbit burrows. Leaves piles of soil as evidence.

= *Rattus norvegicus*: Introduced Brown Rat aka Sewer Rat or Street Rat

Brown Rat

Scat

Reproduced by Permission of Oxford University Press Australia and New Zealand from a Field Guide to Mammals of Australia by Peter Menkhorst and Frank Knight © 2001 Frank Knight

IDENTIKIT 3

Scat: similar in shape to Brown Rat but fatter and lighter brown, and longer.

Appearance: stocky body. HB 120-200 mm. Dark brown feet with black soles. Blackish-brown fur above, long and soft. Dull yellow to grey below.

Tail: shorter than body length, naked, dark grey or blackish, rings of scales.

Habitat and nest: wet, grassy places on the east coast. Builds 1 m deep burrows with narrow entrance. Sometimes build burrows in gardens but it's *nothing* to worry about. They're harmless.

= *Rattus lutreolus*: native Swamp Rat

Swamp Rat

Scat

Reproduced by Permission of Oxford University Press Australia and New Zealand from a Field Guide to Mammals of Australia by Peter Menkhorst and Frank Knight © 2001 Frank Knight

IDENTIKIT 4

Scat: torpedo shaped or slightly bent, 17 mm long, dark. Usually pointed at one end. Smells like rotting plants.
Appearance: rounded ears. Grey to red brown fur above, grey-cream below. Pinkish brown feet, pale soles. HB 100-125 mm. Often mistaken for the Black Rat.
Tail: roughly equal to body length, naked, pinkish-brown or grey, rings of overlapping scales.
Habitat and nest: forest, woodlands and scrub along most of the east and south-west coasts. Small burrows 2-3 m long, often near tree bases.
= ***Rattus fuscipes*****: native Bush Rat**

Bush Rat

Scat

IDENTIKIT 5

Scat: cylinder broken into pieces.
Appearance: HB 300-390 mm. Upper parts greyish-brown to rich golden brown, underparts cream to golden-orange. Small nostrils, eyes and ears set high on the head. Hind feet partly webbed – an adaptation for swimming. Smells musky.
Tail: the white-tipped tail is an excellent way to tell this species apart from others. Very long tail – 230-300 mm, thickly furred, dark grey or blackish. Thickly built, acting like a rudder to help steer in the water.
Habitat and nest: creeks, rivers, lakes, islands. Burrows in creek banks with large front doors up to 15 cm wide.
= ***Hydromys chryogaster*****: native Water Rat**

Water Rat

Scat

IDENTIKIT 6

Scat: small, brown, pointed at one end, 4 mm long with musty smell.
Appearance: small head and long, narrow snout with long thin whiskers.
Tail: as long as the body. Pinkish-brown and naked except for a few short hairs.
Habitat and nest: found everywhere (except rainforests), especially where people are. Builds a sphere-shaped nest of rags, bark and paper sometimes in the middle of a burrow with several entrances. Likes to nest in roofs, behind skirting boards, in woodpiles or haystacks.
= ***Mus musculus*: Introduced House Mouse**

House Mouse

Scat

THE PROSECUTION

'Thank you for the excellent forensic evidence,' the judge said. 'Now I call the main witness to the stand. I know you didn't witness the act being carried out. But do you recognise any of these scats?'

'Yes Your Honour,' Humph said. 'We kept a sample of the scat left in our kitchen. That *Rattus rattus* scat looks identical to it.'

'What do you have to say for yourself *Rattus rattus*? I remind you of the penalties for perjury.'

'I ain't saying nothing,' Rattus replied. And his cousin *Rattus norvegicus* also refused to speak.

'What say you?' The judge turned to the Swamp Rat.

'I ain't into late night parties Your Honour. And I don't go inside houses either.'

'Me neither,' said Bush Rat.

'I live in creeks. And I'm not into that apple and potato junk food. I'm into fishy-type things. You know lots of healthy Omega 3 stuff,' Water Rat said. 'Your honour while I'm in the witness box may I have a word? I've been elected as spokesperson for we native rats.'

'Our safety is so threatened, especially by foxes, dogs and cats. Please can you get everyone to lock up their cats at night? And get everyone to help by reporting foxes, feral cats and dogs to the local council or National Parks and Wildlife Service. And for goodness sake, the best way to deal with a rodent problem is to contact an *expert* pest controller. Otherwise we innocent guys cop it big time.'

'I will make a strong recommendation to the Ministry of the Environment. Next witness now please. What have you to say, *Mus musculus*? Your name is weird to start with.'

'No way I can leave calling cards *that* big,' House Mouse said. 'Not even if I took laxatives!'

'Line up and open your mouths wide now. I want to compare your teeth with the marks on Exhibit One. Hmm, very interesting.'

'I have reviewed all the evidence and listened to your testimonies. But I have no doubt as to who the perp is. It can't be anyone but you *Rattus rattus*. You have done a terrible deed.'

'These are the charges against you:

- Being an illegal immigrant
- Break and enter
- Destruction of property
- Stealing the false teeth of other rats
- Outcompeting our native rats and mice for food
- Causing people to kill innocent natives.

But I will ensure that you are disposed of kindly, without undue suffering. I sentence you to a life of hard labour in the Siberian salt mines.'

POBBLEBONK DETECTIVE ACTIVITY - BUILDING SUSPECT IDENTIKITS

- Detectives - have you got a rat problem at your place? *Please* tell your parents to check the suspect's identikit before taking any action. Get a line-up organised!
- Collect pictures of native rats and mice to sharpen up your detective observation skills. Display the results at school and home so everyone can learn the differences.
- Which ones might live near you?

IDENTIKIT SKILLS

- Overseas Detectives - it is most likely that you have black and brown rats around. But are there any native look-alikes? Compile their identikits.
- Observe the photo of the water rat and develop an identikit for the Water Rat. Include ear position and shape, body shape, toes, tail shape, colour of the tail tip, and colour of the feet and fur.
- That cute creature, the Bush Rat is commonly mistaken for the Black Rat. Identify at least seven differences between the two. Which main feature sets the Black Rat apart from all others?

IS IT A BLACK RAT?

First look at the behaviour:

- Is the creature active during both day and night and does it seem comfortable around humans?
- Is it a good climber, often seen in fruit trees, scaling fences and electrical wires or the roof of a house?
- Is there a nest in your roof, made of shredded materials such as paper?
- Has it been seen feeding on grains, food scraps, fruit or pet food? If your suspect passes all of these questions then it is a Black Rat.

Next look at the tail

- Each of the rats in the identikits have different tail lengths relative to their bodies.
- The tail of *Rattus rattus* is *clearly* longer than the body. Only *Rattus rattus* and the Water Rat have pinkish coloured tails. But the Water Rat's tail has a white tip.

Lastly

- Look at the overall, shape, size and colour.

WORD GOT AROUND

Word spread far and wide via the 'bush telegraph' about the children's work. A letter post-marked Canberra, arrived from the Department of Environment.

Dear Mathieson Children,

Congratulations! Your work on the two 'Poo Dunnit' cases has earned you the Young Scientist of the Year Award. Your achievements have been widely recognised and will be published in several journals. Please come to Canberra on Australia Day next year to collect your award.

Yours sincerely,

John Best

Director

OZZIE'S BIG NIGHT ARRIVED

SHIDS sent congratulations. However, Horace wrote, you have many tests still to come. But was this SHIDS business for real? Was it Granny pulling a giant hoax? The kids still couldn't decide.

Frogsville reconsidered. Perhaps this *was* important scientific work after all. Ozzie was beside himself with joy at the award. Samantha will be so impressed he thought. No one had seen him this happy for a long time. This was Fee's checklist for his date with her:

- Toenails and fingernails neatly trimmed and cleaned
- Armpit hair trimmed, plenty of deodorant
- Teeth cleaned and flossed, tongue defuzzed
- Hair degreased, neatly cut and combed
- Ears de-waxed and cleaned behind as well
- Best clothes freshly washed and ironed and shoes cleaned.

Ozzie met all the conditions. He no longer looked three quarters of the way to a bad fright Fee thought. He had shed several kilos and looked great. Granny drove the kids over to pick up Samantha. Mrs. Sneddon-Smythe answered the door.

'How are you all? Have you had a good week? It's most exciting about your award!'

'We've had a great time,' Pete gushed. 'First of all we finally solved Poo Dunnit over

at Humph's. You know, we've been catching rats for weeks and…...' Fee dug him in the ribs before he totally blew it for Ozzie.

'And I'm going to pursue a career with Scotland Yard,' Ozzie beamed, puffing out his chest.

Samantha looked at him adoringly, even smiling at Fee. She no longer cared that Fee had beaten her in the exams. All she could think about was Ozzie.

How would it all go? Well *of course*, what would you expect? It wasn't long before all hell broke loose on the Frogsville Front. And who do you think was responsible?